The Spectrum Series in Humanistic Psychology, edited by Rollo May and Charles Hampden-Turner, aims to present those psychological viewpoints that place the human being at the organizing center of social reality. It assumes that persons have potential for growth and unfolding in relationship with others, that the ideas they hold about themselves have important consequences, at least partly self-fulfilling. Human beings are free to choose, yet choices once made have determinable, and sometimes inexorable, results, for which the social scientist must share responsibility. In short, we posit an unbreakable relationship between the knower and the known to which each contributes.

We present this series in the hope that a science of the human being will evolve which is worthy of the humanistic tradition and the richness of human endowments.

ROLLO MAY
CHARLES HAMPDEN-TURNER
General Editors

PETER KOESTENBAUM is Professor of Philosophy at San José State University in California. He has received the statewide Outstanding Professor Award of the California State University and Colleges and is an associate director of the Psychological Studies Institute of Palo Alto, California. His other books include *The Vitality of Death: Essays in Psychology and Philosophy* and *Existential Sexuality* (Prentice-Hall).

MANAGING ANXIETY

the power of knowing who you are

PETER KOESTENBAUM

A SPECTRUM BOOK

Prentice-Hall, Inc., Englewood Cliffs, New Jersey

Library of Congress Cataloging in Publication Data

KOESTENBAUM, PETER
  Managing anxiety
  (Spectrum series in humanistic psychology)

  (A Spectrum Book)
  (1. Anxiety 2. Consciousness I. Title
  (DNLM: 1. Anxiety WM172 K78m)
BF575. A6K6   616.8'52   74–8555
ISBN 0–13–550350–7
ISBN 0–13–550343–4 (pbk)

We are grateful to the following publishers for their permission to quote from the works listed below:

To Little, Brown and Company and George Allen and Unwin Ltd., for permission to reprint the Frontispiece "To Edith," from *The Autobiography of Bertrand Russell.* Copyright 1951, 1952, 1953, 1956 by Bertrand Russell. Copyright © 1961 by Allen and Unwin Ltd. Copyright © 1967 by George Allen and Unwin Ltd.

To Seabury Press and Ediciones Carlos Lohlé, for permission to reprint a selection from Ernesto Cardenal's *To Live Is to Love,* translated by Kurt Reinhardt. Ediciones Carlos Lohlé is the publisher of the original Spanish-language version, *Vida en el Amor.*

NOTE: The names, places, and identifying circumstances of the illustrative materials in this book have been changed to protect the anonymity of my students. Diana is not a real person, but is a collage, as is her letter, derived from those of several women.

PRENTICE-HALL INTERNATIONAL, INC. (*London*)
PRENTICE-HALL OF AUSTRALIA PTY., LTD. (*Sydney*)
PRENTICE-HALL OF CANADA, LTD. (*Toronto*)
PRENTICE-HALL OF INDIA PRIVATE LIMITED (*New Delhi*)
PRENTICE-HALL OF JAPAN, INC. (*Tokyo*)

Contents

*This book is dedicated to
my private students in philosophy*

*Special thanks are due to
Michael Hunter, Robert Heidel, and Jean Homan
for their support, acumen, and assistance
in the preparation of this book.*

Behold a good doctrine
has been given you;
forsake it not

Proverbs 4:2

Introduction:

Philosophy
Is for Everyone

What You Will Find
in This Book

This book rests on two closely interconnected ideas. You will learn about the nature of human consciousness and discover how that knowledge can help you in the management of anxiety. Anxiety has many forms and it comes to plague all of us. I use the word "pain" (or sometimes "suffering") to designate all the negative aspects of life—that is, those aspects usually thought to be undesirable.

Philosophy, traditionally, has been assigned the task of helping us with the anxieties that are inevitable accompaniments of life. An important branch of philosophy today—sometimes called phenomenology or existentialism, but also having its roots in the many varieties of Eastern thought (Zen, Buddhism, Vedanta, etc.)—seeks to fulfill that ancient philosophic duty. The principal area of investigation of this popular and relevant form of philosophy today is the study of the nature of human consciousness. In fact, the study of human consciousness is prerequisite to understanding any and all applications of philosophy to human problems. The human problem area that concerns us in this book is anxiety.[1] As a consequence, we will have to first examine that mysterious entity which goes under the name of consciousness or awareness and then explore how we can handle constructively the pain of anxiety.

The book is divided for convenience into two parts corresponding to the two topics which unify it.

1 See also my companion volume, *Existential Sexuality*.

How To Use This Book

Philosophy is the most ancient of the healing arts.

This book is your personal guide to understanding the existential philosophic life. It is best you read it through from the beginning. I therefore ask you to be patient with this book. I also feel confident that your efforts will be well rewarded.

This book is like a tall building. It builds up the existential philosophic life step by step. First you see your plans, then you build your steel frame and your scaffolding. Only then are you ready to add walls, floors, and the windows that look out into the world. In the end, you are ready to do your furnishing and interior decorating, those additions that mean comfort and pleasure. Then, of course, you move in!

The ideas build on each other. You will understand the section on pain better if you have first read the section on the field of consciousness theory of man.

As you read these pages, you should build up your intellectual understanding of what constitutes a conscious human being. But throughout you should be aware that these ideas must be put into practice. You must experience personally what you read.

Look upon the people discussed in the many illustrations herein as your friends: They are like members of a supportive encounter group or an accepting family. We all at times feel ourselves adrift and searching for a shoreline, imploring others' help; it is our common agony that gives us our sense of brotherhood.

Always remember: Philosophy is the central business of life. Everything follows from your philosophical world view. Therapy and medicine, money and success, and all similar values are but adjuncts to your basic philosophy of man. They are the dress of existence; philosophy is the bones, sinews, and muscles. Philosophy is the center. Existential philosophy represents our pursuit of the authentic meaning of human fulfillment. Every one of us needs a philosophy of life. The more competent and thoughtful we are, the more accurate is our philosophy of life, and the more successful will it be to sustain, protect, and guide us.

The motto of this book—the compassionate understanding of human beings—could well be summed up in the following passage from Bertrand Russell's autobiography:

Love and knowledge, so far as they were possible, led upward toward the heavens. But always pity brought me back to earth. Echoes of cries of pain reverberate in my heart. Children in famine, victims tortured by oppressors, helpless old people a hated burden to their sons, and the whole world of loneliness, poverty, and pain make a mockery of what human life should be. I long to alleviate the evil, but I cannot, and I too suffer.[2]

Pity is not enough. Philosophy must demonstrate that it has an aggressive program for the conquest of suffering—both for individuals and for society.

Everyone Needs a Home

Philosophy can help the homeless find a home. Every man needs a home. A home is a part of the universe that belongs permanently to one individual person. You need a home, an eternally protective slice of the cosmos as your very own. You need to be anchored, so that no power on earth nor in the heavens above can ever dislodge you. A true home should protect you against such dangers as attack, injustice, and theft, and also against poverty, hunger, anxiety, disease, old age, and even against death. An authentic home is like a warm mother: it soothes your pain, wipes your tears, quenches your thirst, and feeds your hunger. A genuine home is like God creating Adam, because a true home defines you: It tells you who you are; it gives you an identity. It makes you unique; it gives you individuality.

For example, at one time you may have asked yourself, "Am I to be sensitive, artistic, delicate, and endowed with deep feelings? Or am I to be a rough, tough, single-minded pioneering type?" A true home will answer that question for you, because it determines your values and describes your roles in life. You undoubtedly have asked yourself "Am I treating my parents (or my children, my spouse, or myself) as I should? Is my conscience clear, or do I feel guilt about the way I behave toward them?" What is right? To declare your independence and tell your mother to leave you alone or to decide to be a loyal son or daughter and invite her to live with you or even to move in with her? Your true home answers that question for you with absolute certainty and authority; it informs you what you must do to resolve your guilts. A true home will tell you precisely, in every specific situation, what your duty is to your parents, yourself, your children, and how the conflicts that arise should be resolved. A true home informs you of your precise duties to your country, to God, and to each one of your fellow men.

A true home gives you correct answers about what is the right personality for you. "Should I drift or should I achieve?" "Should I conform or be independent?" "Should I be an introverted poet or an extraverted athlete?" "Should I live for the now or for the future?"

2 *The Autobiography of Bertrand Russell* (Boston: Little, Brown and Co., 1967), p. 4.

For pleasure or for duty?" A home responds to these questions and thus relieves you of anxiety and guilt. What makes a home your home is your knowledge that the answers are true. A home is also where you find the bliss of forgiveness. A home will always take you back and always love you, if you return, surrender, and confess your trespasses.

Now ask yourself, with naked honesty and innocent candor, "Do *I* have answers to life's important questions?" "Does it hurt me not to have answers?" "Does it pain me if whatever answers I do have are neither certain nor accurate?" If you have answers, you have a home. Chances are, if you are reading this book, you probably do not have answers you can rely on in final matters concerning life and death. And if you do not have answers then you do not have a home, though you know at the same time that such a home is an absolute necessity.

Philosophy is the search for that home—a search without illusions. Today a concern with existential philosophy can make us aware that this home is no longer found in places where our ancestors once believed they discovered it—the farm, the family, the church, the country, the flag, the party, the cause, etc. Traditional avenues of finding a home have failed dismally and continue to fail. And attempts to maintain a stiff upper lip—the aggressive facade of the pseudo-adult —produce symptoms but not security, create anaesthesia but not authenticity.

Examples

Modern civilization has made man homeless. Perhaps it is more accurate to say that man has for the most part always been homeless, but that the technological explosion of this century has forced most of us to become painfully aware of the real meaning of that relentless homelessness. We might say that men of previous ages were blessed with blindness about this lack. Today parents divorce and leave their children without the family they were born into. The primary home is thus destroyed permanently, and children thus receive their first lesson in homelessness. Similarly, society dictates that children eventually leave their parents' home to make a life for themselves. As a consequence, neither parents nor children are the same when (and if) they do meet again. They become strangers, often losing forever the connection that meant home to them. Thus, as children grow up, they get free instruction in alienation. Nor does closeness to the land offer any succor. Many a person has traveled back to the land of his ancestors hoping to recapture there his true home. He has always been disappointed, because being uprooted from the soil is being a tree separated from its nourishment, and that is a lesson in starvation.

Jerry, a black student whose family came from Alabama, thought he could find his true home by taking a trip to Ghana, with the possibility of settling there permanently. Although he felt he was a stranger in the U.S., he believed he would achieve a profound feeling of homecoming when he arrived in Africa. Unfortunately it did not work out that way for Jerry. As a matter of fact, he was even more of a stranger in Accra than in San Francisco. It took him a long and expensive trip to make the philosophical discovery of all contemporary individuals: that man, though desperately in need of a home, does not have one merely by virtue of being born into a family, a race, a nation.

Ruben has a similar story to tell. His family emigrated from Poland to America during the Nazi persecution of Jews in World War II. His yearning for his ancestral home is seen in the fact that he has never lost his Polish accent nor his fluency in Yiddish. He finally managed to make his pilgrimage to Jerusalem. Arriving at the Wailing Wall at last, where he thought he was going to find his true home, he wept; but he wept not with joy because he was home, but with the darkest anguish because he now knew that his home was nowhere in the tangible world. After the Wailing Wall, no other place was left to look for home. It cost him a heartbreaking experience to discover in his own life—in his flesh, blood, and bones—the philosophic truth that human beings are homeless. This tragic knowledge may mean little when expounded theoretically in a philosophy book; but it means a great deal if experienced as ultimate disappointment and dark emptiness at the Wailing Wall in Jerusalem.

Paul, recently divorced, went back to the Kansas farm of his parents having lived in Vancouver, Canada, most of his life. But rather than finding there his true home he found a couple of strangers in a land he had never really known.

John and Cindy took to the wilderness. They went homesteading in Alaska in search of man's authentic ancestral home. They lived romantically and wrote like Thoreau. But did they find a true home? Their bodies relaxed and their health improved, but it was only the envy of those they left behind that supported their wavering conviction that indeed they had found their home. John and Cindy ultimately discovered that, far from finding a home, they had brought their homelessness with them all the way north to Alaska. Their original question was, Could the problem of homelessness—which resisted all solutions in Boston—be solved in Alaska instead? Their answer was "no."

History and culture are filled with ersatz homes, with phony roots, and with surrogate foundations.

There are myths and rituals, prejudices and clichés which try to lull us into believing there does exist a home for us. A very religious person may feel that rigorous and mechanical adherence to dietary laws, liturgy, prayers, rituals, and church attendance will in fact provide this home. But many an educated, modern person can no longer be adequately satisfied with such a mechanical approach; neither his intellect nor his emotions permit him to exchange compulsive behavior for an authentic home. A contemporary enlightened individual rightfully doubts that his home can really be found in ritual and dogma. The rugged American complete with trailer, gun, and boat may hope that reminiscing about his pioneer past and mimicking the life of an early American, while at the same time perceiving himself from the vantage point of a late twentieth-century American suburbanite, will provide a home for him. Instead he is apt to get mosquito bites and debts; he is as homeless as before. The most he can hope for, if indeed his camping has esthetic content for him, is that in the solitude of the High Sierras or in the misty expanse of the Pacific Ocean (which Alan Watts called the edge of the world) he will confront and touch that abysmal aloneness, that singular point which is man's deliciously purified and agonizingly ecstatic recognition of his essential homelessness. Perhaps with these almost unbearable realizations he can begin to find his true home through the philosophic pursuit of the nature of his being.

There exists much advertising that promises to take you home, to give you a home, if only you buy a certain brand of cigarettes, whiskey, deodorant, or clothing. Such advertising is fraudulent and cynical, because it does not inform or deliver but instead preys on a real need. Even the actual purchase of a home is confused with this basic human need. Too many believe that the transactions in a real estate office are in some way connected to their foundation need for a true home. Before the purchase such a man may have been a *wandering* searcher for a home; he is now a mortgage-bound *stationary* searcher for a home. Too many people are ensnared and enslaved by real estate —under the illusion that they fell in love with the view, the neighborhood, the floor plan, the kitchen, or the tax advantages—into believing that the human problem of homelessness can be managed through a thirty- or forty-year-long indebtedness. If anything at all is achieved, it is that the *distraction* from the real problem is now made permanent. What a pity, especially if we consider that this is the only life we are likely to have!

Answers

Let us now look at some solutions. Philosophy, especially as the existential way of life, can deal with the problem of our home. The basic message of responsible existential philosophy in answer to the problem of alienation is this: *the dependable and imperishable home exists in the individual, subjective, and inward spirit of every human being.* And by the generic expression "existential philosophy" I mean all of those contemporary philosophical views that study the structure and the health of that miraculous and mysterious phenomenon which we call human consciousness.

Home is the consciousness that each of us is in our silent and solitary centers. It is the consciousness that is aroused when two individuals meet in love, not in sex. Home is the consciousness that is in touch with the cosmic stream, that senses its oneness with the life of the universe itself. To understand and to experience that individual conscious center is to have found our home. That insight can be integrated into all aspects of life. And that is our task—to show that this home can be found and it can be shared. We can live there and thus find the true meaning of the dignity and the brotherhood of man. The path home is through philosophy, through insight and introspection into consciousness, and not exclusively through the technological manipulation of our material environment. We cannot come home through the expenditure of vast sums of money or expensive moves, or through divorces and gadgets, but only through the discovery of our sacred inward nature.

It is not necessary to be a professional philosopher to understand these issues and their attempted answers. In fact, familiarity with the philosophical foundations of these insights is no guarantee that one will in fact discover his true home and live there, any more than the study of medicine produces health or the study of economics produces wealth. Each of us needs to build for himself a livable philosophy of man.

Philosophy Can Help You Without Your Becoming a Philosopher

People with problems (that means all of us) today turn for help to psychiatry, psychology, medicine, and pharmacology. It is less common for us to take our troubles to philosophy for help. Philosophy, however, is the oldest of all the healing arts. The accumulated wisdom of philosophy, especially the existential philosophy that has developed professionally in recent decades, can serve as a basis for resolving many of our daily problems—such as success, love, and raising children, as well as such problems as anxiety, guilt, and depression. Moreover, not all problems are signs of "illness." There are stresses and other problems that are symptoms of health. It is the task of philosophy to help us, not with our diseases, but with our condition of health. The inevitable fact of anxiety is a case in point. Medicine can alleviate anxiety; philosophy can give meaning to anxiety. Drugs can allay suffering but they cannot produce either meaning or love.

The everyday use of philosophy for the purpose of enhancing one's life and solving its deepest problems is as old as Socrates and ancient Tibet but also as new as space exploration. The general benefits of medicine, psychiatry, psychology, and pharmacology have been widely publicized and have been made generally available. Philosophy, infinitely older than these sciences, has mostly been the property of those introduced to its scholarly technicalities and conceptual intricacies. The general public senses, accurately, a great philosophic vacuum and demands, justifiably, that this emptiness be filled. Today, a vast communication gap exists between the insights of a "professional on human nature" and the so-called general public. This gap is both unhealthy and unfair. Other sciences have bridged this gap; it is now necessary for philosophy to do the same.

You know that medicine and chemistry as well as psychology and engineering can help to make a better life for you. But what can philosophy do for you? Do you know that the real issues, the deepest issues in your life—the issues that precede all others—can only be handled with philosophy, not with engineering, physics, or psychiatry? Medicine cannot save you from death—it can only postpone the end. Philosophy can help you deal successfully with that inevitable limit to your life. Psychiatry can cure a phobia but it cannot deal with the philosophical problem of how to manage your free will and the anxiety and responsibility that accompany it. Psychiatry cannot eliminate the anguish that comes from freedom in making choices—it can only ameliorate the pathological expressions of that anguish. Philosophy can show you how anguish can teach the philosophic truth about man to you. In fact, you need philosophy far more than technology in order to know what it means to live well. That point is forgotten in the desperate speed and chaos of the modern world.

The Two Emergencies in Your Life

In life there are two kinds of emergency: sickness and health. In our society we tend to recognize as real only the first of these. Sickness means pain, often unbearable pain. Here is our first emergency. We then run to a healer for help. We believe that once the pain is stilled we are truly healed.

However, what is usually called "health" is but a beginning, never an end. When we are in good physical and mental health we have not concluded our life's destiny. On the contrary, we have merely equipped ourselves to move on to the second emergency: how to live well, how to fulfill our destiny, and how to give our life true meaning.

John B. has devoted the first half-century of his life to developing a successful restaurant chain. He has devoted all of his physical and psychological powers to business success. That was his response to the first emergency—his specific and individual pain was his lack of financial security. His goal—a substantial and secure income—has now been attained. Having reached this destination, John B. discovers that meeting his first emergency leads to his second emergency, expressed in the question, What is the meaning of life? In a way, John B. is now ready for his second career, in the sense in which all people, upon entering the second half of their lives, are ready for philosophy. But what is that career to be? He has prepared himself for *something*, it seems, during his first fifty years. But what is that evasive "something" for which all this extraordinary preparation is intended? Many who, having concluded this period of "preparation" in life and having achieved what appears to outsiders as the culmination of their careers, face now their *second* emergency—and become lost. John's second emergency is the question of what will give significance to his life. How should he use his newly acquired freedom? How can he meet his eventual death? How can he conquer, or accommodate himself to, the inexorable movement of time? Of what value are his accomplishments when all values are called in question and when all life ends in death anyway?

Philosophy is the only science that addresses itself specifically to that second emergency.

Exercise

Here is a brief introductory exercise for you, the reader. Reflect on the following questions and give serious answers to them, preferably in writing. You may begin, in this way, a journal that should accompany your readings and reflections in the existential way of life.

Do you think that the second emergency is deeper than the first? Do you think you should answer the second emergency—the problem of meaning in life—before you handle the first—financial solvency? Do you think that failure to deal with the first emergency is but an escape from facing the second and much more serious emergency? As long as life is pain, as long as you must watch calories to control your weight, swallow pills to control your blood pressure, work sixteen hours a day to establish financial freedom, as long as all these efforts are needed to meet your first emergency, there can be no time to handle the second. Do you experience that as a relief? The first emergency has answers—you can consult the experts: doctors, therapists, economists, educators, etc. But does the second emergency have answers? The second emergency is deeper and more important than the first. "Success" in life may really be an escape from philosophy. What do *you* think?

1:

Metaphors
for Consciousness

Our consciousness shapes our ego and our world. Some concepts of the ego and of the world confuse and obscure the notion of consciousness itself, other ego-concepts and world-concepts facilitate our understanding of the *intentional character* of consciousness. To explain this theory, we describe what the phenomenologist Edmund Husserl referred to as the *ego-cogitum-cogitatum* structure of consciousness. All conscious acts—that is, all experiences of being—have an *I* as their core (*ego*), which reaches out through perception, volition, knowledge, etc. (*cogito*) to an object (*cogitatum*). That threefold structure characterizes the essence of the field of consciousness; it is a description of the *intentionality of consciousness*.

At this point it would be helpful to clarify the meaning of consciousness by listing some of the metaphors I have used with my students. The following chapter will clarify two concepts of consciousness that shape the individual's personality and environment. Then, with a general idea of the nature of human consciousness as developed by an existential philosophy, we will be ready to consider how such a view can be applied to the problems of living.

The specific features of consciousness that I attempt to illustrate through these metaphors include the following: (1) Consciousness is continuous with but different from its objects in the world. These objects range from such presumably subjective objects as feelings, ideas and concepts to objects usually acknowledged as such, including human bodies, trees and planets. (2) The relation between subject and object, consciousness and the world—or, in the language of traditional philosophy, the mind-body connection—is of the order of a *field*. On the one end (the subjective end) the field is, as it were, diaphanous, transparent, like a void. On the other end, the field is solid and concrete. There is no specific border in which mind becomes matter. The area of connection is more like a gradually thickening fog. The region symbolized by the void is called consciousness or subjectivity, whereas the region symbolized by concreteness is called world or objectivity. (3) I believe that we know the truth of the field theory of consciousness through direct and unprejudiced inspection of the general nature of our human experience. That approach when made systematic is called, in philosophy, the phenomenological method. Finally, (4) the consequences of this view are both dramatic and health producing. Let me now turn to the metaphors.

1. *Man is a river.* The life of each individual man is like a river; like a space probe, ever flowing into the space beyond and into the time of the future. It is more accurate and therefore better to say that man is a river that flows than to say he is a body that is static. Man is more like a space capsule hurtling into the future than a grouping of molecules forming a society of cells. Man's sense of flowing union with nature and with the universe is a more accurate description of him than his belief that he exists separated from the world around him.

Magnets and Comets

2. *The field-of-consciousness theory.* The life of each individual man is an amorphous *field,* a process and a continuum rather than a thing with clear limits or an object with sharp boundaries. Specifically, a human being is like a magnetic field, where the positive and negative poles are, respectively, man the subject and man the object, man as consciousness and man as the world, man as mind and man as body, and man as awareness and man as behavior.

Important consequences follow from this analogy. For one, the mind is not "in" the body, just as the magnet's positive pole is not "in" its negative pole. The mind is outside the body in the same sense that the positive pole is outside the negative pole. Finally, to continue with our metaphor, the existence of the body is dependent on and brought about by the existence of the mind in the same way that the existence of the negative pole of the magnet is dependent on and brought about by the existence of the positive pole. A positive pole—as is the case with a positive electrical charge—automatically and instantaneously creates an equal and opposing charge beyond and outside itself.

The metaphor of the magnet must be taken seriously. The idea of a field, used prevalently in physics, is made possible by the fact that man's existence in this world is a continuous and bipolar field rather than a collection of isolated objects or things. I do not think that the converse is true—namely, that the field theory of consciousness is grafted onto an image borrowed from physics or from farming (as in "a wheat field"). The field of consciousness theory of man transforms radically our ideas about the relation between mind and body.

3. *Man and his world.* A fish is nothing without its ecosystem and man is nothing without his world. But the fish is not the sea or the aquarium and man is not his world or his body. Man and world, consciousness and objects, like fish and aquarium, are interdependent, but without either of them losing his identity, individuality, uniqueness, independence, and difference.

4. *The comet theory.* Closely following on the conceptions embraced by the field-of-consciousness theory is the idea that all things therefore exist only and always in a field of perception. And perception is a manifestation of consciousness. We can call this fact the *comet theory of objects.* Each object—whether it be a tree or a cloud, an idea or a feeling, my body or my behavior (all of which are objects to my consciousness)—is like a flaming comet, attached to which is a long and luminous tail. Similarly, every object is not merely a thing that exists by itself but also has attached to it a "tail" or a stream of consciousness. A tree is not simply a tree, but it is a tree-seen-by-an-observer. And my experience, of course, discloses that this observer is always "I." A mathematical concept is not the bare concept but a concept-thought-by-a-person. If I think of a person perceiving a tree, then the tree is really a tree-observed-by-a-person-observed-by-me. Moreover, I-observe-an-observer-observing-a-mathematical-concept; that is the total nature of a concept. Everything you perceive in the universe has a string attached to it that connects directly to you. The tether is always there although sometimes it is tenuous and can be experientially detected only through meditation practices or what in philosophy is called a transcendental-phenomenological reduction, a stepping back *into* consciousness and *out of* involvement with life.

Family Therapy

The comet theory of objects has been successfully applied to a kind of psychotherapy called existential family counseling. A San Diego, California, therapist uses a large plastic cube with transparent windows on each of its six sides, which serves to illustrate the point that every object or event (such as a family situation) has many subjective sides to it. And unless we get a *complete* picture we do not get any picture at all. The cube suggests that so-called objective solutions to family problems represent an unreal quest. The individual subjective perceptions must be included in any family argument before we have a real or true picture of the actual situation. Each one of the six transparent windows of the cube is of a different color. Inside, in the center of the cube, is affixed a small globe with the outlines of the continents and the oceans clearly visible. That globe represents the family as an object (or any other object, up to and including the whole world), which is seen in several different ways, represented in the cube by the variously colored windows. As you look through any of the individually colored transparent plastic windows you can see the globe as well as the remaining five windows. As you shift from one transparent window to another, you notice that the globe changes color with the changing color of each new window and that the colors of the other visible windows also change. In other words, each window provides a particular, individualized, and different coloration of both the world and of each of the other windows to that same world.

The Comet Theory
as Applied in Psychotherapy

When the Smith family visited this therapist he used the cube in the following way. Mrs. Smith had initially come in for counseling because her second girl, thirteen-year-old Evelyn, had become increasingly more intractable at home. "The entire family is in a constant uproar because of Evelyn," she said. The therapist suggested that all four family members come in for counseling. The whole family, not Evelyn alone, had a problem.

The first step in his therapy was to ask each family member to develop his own diagnosis of the total family situation. "What is the matter with the family?" the therapist asked each member in turn. Everyone of course had a different opinion. Thomas, the father, felt that his wife, Ethel, did not spend enough time with Evelyn. "Ethel is never home when Evelyn returns from school, and she expects me, after a hard day at the plant, to take care of the problem," he complained. Teresa, Evelyn's fifteen-year-old sister, felt that Evelyn needed more discipline than she had been getting because, as Teresa put it, "Evelyn always interferes with everything I do. She listens in on my phone calls, she turns the TV on high when I do homework, she wakes me up early in the mornings on weekends, and so on." And Evelyn herself could only cry and mutter, "No one understands me" when she was asked to diagnose the family's needs.

The therapist then took a crayon and wrote a different family member's name over each one of the windows of the cube. Over the fifth window he wrote his own name and over the sixth he simply wrote "Grandma." "Let's find out what troubles this family," he started. Then he asked, "What does this family truly look like?"

"The family, you think, is the small globe inside. The globe looks different to each one of you. Look!" And he asked each member to view the family (small globe) and its other members (windows) and then to describe to the others what he saw. Obviously, everyone saw something different. He then added, "It also looks different to Grandma and different to me."

The lesson the therapist was teaching is that there exists no objective family reality; there exists in this world no object that can be called "the Smith family." There exist only a series of subject-object fields, relations, and connections. The *problem*—experienced as emotional pain—is the mistaken belief that the family is a thing. The *solution*—experienced as relief, resolution, and joy—is the knowledge that the family is a series of subject-object fields, each of which is partially the same as the others and partially different from them.

A family is a conglomerate of subjective ways of perceiving the common object "family" (the small globe) *and* the uncommon subjectivities of the other family members (the other windows). We must remember that each object has a conscious or subjective tail or string attached to it. Even though there is only *one* globe (one family), there are six window-globe combinations. The true family is not the uniform central globe but the sum of the six window-globe combinations.

In this way the therapist introduces a decent respect for the legitimacy of each one of the family's personal centers and for the reality of each individual subjective perspective. Such a new way of perceiving a family structure, within the context of a field-of-consciousness theory of man, creates a healthy respect for one's own needs and an ethical toleration for the needs of others.

The therapist can now point out to Mrs. Smith that what appears to her as a serious problem does not seem that way at all to him. Mrs. Smith's window colors the family "troubled," whereas the therapist's window colors it "normal." Thomas' window colors the family as "burdensome," whereas Evelyn's window colors the family as "unfair." Furthermore, Mrs. Smith's window colors Evelyn's window as "guilty and irresponsible," while Evelyn's window colors Mrs. Smith's window as "insensitive" and even as "hateful." As a consequence of this analysis, the family atmosphere changed from one of domination and control to one of letting be, from rigidity to freedom.

Additional Metaphors

5. *Consciousness and body.* The mind-body and man-world boundaries are like a beach. The beach is an ambiguous and interpenetrating, oscillating boundary between land and sea. Land and sea are precisely defined and conspicuously different from each other. Yet their boundary is always unclear and always changing—quickly with the waves and slowly with the tides. The same is true of the mind-body, consciousness-world, and man-environment separation. As the sea is unlike the land, so consciousness is unlike the body; but as sea and land together make a single beach, so consciousness and body unify to make a single person.

6. *Man is a sunburst.* We move now from what has been a series of linear metaphors to circular and spherical ones. Man is a field like a sunburst; he is a field like the solar system. Man's silent consciousness is the super-heated center of the sun. His actions and perceptions, his feelings and aspirations, his thoughts and his hopes, his language, his breath, and his vision are the rays radiating expansively into the vastness of space. And finally, man's body, his behavior, his society, his beliefs, his people, and his world are the objects that are illuminated by this light.

If the solar system could think and if it were as philosophically ignorant as men, it would believe that it is only comprised of the planets. It would think that its total nature is the planets alone. It would be completely unaware of the sun and its rays that make the illumination of the planets possible in the first place.

The total sunburst is the complete solar system—sun, rays, and planets—and not just the planets on its periphery. And the total man is not his body or his world, but the total sunburst, the total consciousness-body-world field.

7. *Man and explosion.* Man is a field like an explosion. He is first of all the center which is empty, evacuated, hollow. He is, second, the flying shrapnel, the onrushing air, and the expanding shockwaves. Third and finally, he is the target, the crater in the ground, or the collapsed structure. The total explosion is the total field from center to target. Similarly, the total man is the total field from inner consciousness to external body, society, and world. In both of these latter metaphors I have made allusion to the theory of intentional consciousness, as described in Chapter 3.

8. *Man is time.* The field of consciousness that is man is also our experience of time. The experience of the forward movement of time is identical with the experience of the growth, forward movement, and futurization of our consciousness. Human consciousness and the experience of time are synonymous. They can serve to clarify and illustrate each other.

As time moves, so does consciousness; both emerge from a past, through a present, into the future. One is called the passage of time and the other is called growth, transcendence, process and fulfillment.

Time does not occur, exist, or flow "in" something, like a matrix, or "on" something, like a base. It may be true that time is a river. But the metaphor is forced. A river has a bed on which it flows. Time has no such bed. Time is ultimate and irreducible. Time cannot be perceived from a perspective that is outside of time. Unlike the river, there can be for time no movement or emergence prior to time or more basic than time or in which time takes place. Time cannot be explained in terms of more primitive concepts; in fact, life is time, the universe is time.

Lived time, experienced time—unlike its meaning in modern physics—is not produced by measurement. On the contrary, measurement makes sense only because to be means to be temporal, to be means to be time. Measurement is a phenomenon that occurs *in* time. What applies to time is also true of the field that is our individual consciousness. Consciousness does not exist *in* something else nor as a product *of* something else. Like time, consciousness is irreducible and primary. Consciousness is certainly not the product of chemical and molecular interactions. On the contrary, these latter can be understood only in and by consciousness. Nor is consciousness the result of a long chain of biological and anthropological evolution. Evolution is a theory constructed by and sustained in consciousness. Consciousness, like time, has always been and always will be. There is no "other" consciousness in which "this" consciousness exists, just as there is no "superior" time or "meta"-time in which "regular" time exists.

There is only time and there is only consciousness, and these are one ultimate.

Time does not have an underlying matrix because it already is the last matrix. It is similar to consciousness; consciousness does not rest on something prior, because it is already the "most" prior aspect of all existence. And temporal consciousness is the field-of-consciousness flow whose running, movement, and energy I experience as *my unique life*.

The psychological equivalent of knowing that I am time is successful living, because success in life means unceasing progress in the process of psychological growth.

Contemporary Consequences

The Ghost-in-a-Machine Theory.   Borrowing a phrase from Gilbert Ryle, the ghost-in-a-machine theory of man views man as an organism or a machine—and nothing else. He operates by the laws of chemistry and mechanics. His mind, consciousness, or soul is not real. It is a ghost hiding insignificantly and half-jokingly somewhere within the wheels and springs and transistors of that machine, or lodged between the organs of that body. According to this view, the mind is the result of chemical events and developments in the brain; culture and human values are the result of thousands of years of anthropological, apelike, behavioral development. There is no understanding whatever about the fact that man is a consciousness, a subjectivity, a unique ego, an inwardness, and even a soul. In my opinion, this theory of man is *false* in that it contradicts the simplest and most obvious facts of human experience. Furthermore, it is *dangerous* because it dehumanizes man by destroying the most precious achievement of his culture —namely, the history of consciousness.

What are the consequences of the ghost-in-a-machine theory of man? Today, this materialistic self-concept is integrated into most of our private and public affairs. Unfortunately, that theory leads to symptom formation. We know how the ghost-in-a-machine theory of man has been tacitly adopted by the society in which we live. It is taught in the schools and it is presupposed in medicine, psychology, and psychiatry. It underlies our political decisions and describes the patterns in which the nation spends its money.

There are, I believe, eight specific consequences that follow from living the ghost-in-a-machine theory of man rather than the field-of-consciousness theory:

1. The "ghost" theory of man expresses itself as *inconsiderateness* in relations among people. It leads to lack of respect for human beings, including oneself. The individual who lives by this theory can-

not perceive another human being as a person, as an inward and unique consciousness. Conversely, he does not perceive himself as a person either. In short, he has no conception of the meaning of personality—in others as well as in himself.

Inconsiderateness may be a small defect compared to the catastrophes brought on by its more extreme and exaggerated forms. But inconsiderateness is the seed which, when fully grown, becomes the cruelty of war.

Crime is such an exaggerated expression of this theory of man, as will be illustrated in the Chapter 2 discussion of Lance and Kelbach. For the criminal, his victim is a thing whose life is meaningless. The philosophical assumption some criminals make is that, just as a cow can be butchered for its meat, so can a citizen be butchered for the contents of his wallet. The criminal is ignorant of the fact that consciousness is sui generis, that the presence of consciousness creates an aura of holiness that is never possessed by objects alone.

An even more exaggerated form of inconsiderateness is terrorism. The terrorist Kozo Okamoto, representing the Popular Front for the Liberation of Palestine, machine-gunned innocent Puerto Rican women and children pilgrims to the Holy Land at Lod International Airport in Tel Aviv in order, ultimately, to establish a new, Maoist, world order. "It is right," for Okamoto and in his own words, "to destroy other human beings for the sake of establishing a new world order in which people will forcefully be rearranged, programmed and reorganized for the sake of their own 'happiness.'" And the nature of happiness is not defined by each individual subjectivity, but by Okamoto.

The final expression of cynical disregard for the integrity of individuals is war. Because any comment on the dehumanizing effects of the kind of inconsiderateness that is war is an understatement, no comment at all is the only proper one. However, war is possible solely because the populations of the warring nations live by a ghost-in-a-machine theory of man. No matter how nations and societies protest about their moral and ethical standing—killing (for example) —they ultimately depend on war and killing to achieve their goals. Our use of war as an instrument of policy presupposes our conviction that men are things (our own men as well as our enemy's). If the two cultures were based on a field-of-consciousness theory of man, empathy for individual subjectivities and sensitivity for the value and integrity of each living consciousness would take precedence over any killing and destruction. "Make love, not war," when translated into the language of philosophy, becomes "Recognize the truth (in the sense of corresponding to the facts of actual experience) of the field-of-consciousness theory of man and the error of the ghost-in-a-machine theory of man."

2. A second consequence of having integrated the ghost-in-a-machine theory of man into the life of our society is that it has killed love. It creates the inability to love by confusing love with the mechanics of sexual petting, physical manipulation, intercourse, and various uses of perversions. It leads to the confusion of true love with role-playing that is thoroughly empty, shallow, energy-consuming, and eventually boring and unsatisfying.

Love is a relationship of meeting on the level of pure consciousness. In love, it is not two bodies that meet, nor is it two roles. In love, two inward subjectivities meet. That kind of meeting requires both to have access to and understanding of their subjective, inward consciousness. Love makes man complete. If he thinks of himself as a thing only—and thinks of others as things for manipulation only—then love is definitely not one of the joys to which he has access.

Love also means to decide to care for another. It means to make a commitment *to* the other, for the welfare *of* the other. He who loves can say, "I have chosen to *care* about what happens to you because I see in you a true human inwardness and because I am also a human subjective consciousness." These insights make sense only in a field-of-consciousness theory of man; within the parameters of a ghost-in-a-machine theory they are incomprehensible and meaningless.

3. The ghost-in-a-machine theory of man, if integrated into life, results in the inability to really communicate with others and share with them. Through the operation of a materialistic and object-oriented self-concept one loses the capacity to be *with* others. In the context of this theory, the only relation to people that is possible is one of manipulation for use, for profit, for individual advancement, and for the accumulation of power, status, and success.

To illustrate both this and the other consequences of the "ghost" theory, consider this example. Grayson is an advancing executive in the aerospace industry. He is personnel manager of the large research department of a western airplane and space equipment manufacturer. On the morning of October 1, Grayson had a choice to make: (1) Visit and hold the hand of his six-year-old daughter, in the hospital after a routine tonsillectomy, or (2) please his boss by attending an important awards breakfast being held for the employees over whom he as personnel manager has jurisdiction. To choose to be with his daughter meant to choose a meeting of two inwardnesses, perhaps through the touch of two hands. It would have been the meeting of the anxious, tired, but loving consciousness of a father with the consciousness of his pained, lonely, anguished, and speechless daughter, a meeting effected by a connecting glance or by the gentle touch of two contacting hands.

On the other hand, to choose to be with his boss meant a positive and almost certain step toward further advancement. Attendance at the awards breakfast would have meant that Grayson pleased his boss, demonstrated his importance and his skill to the other employees, and participated in an important aspect of the company's personnel operations. Grayson's relationship with the child represents the field-of-consciousness theory, whereas the corporation in this context represents the ghost-in-a-machine theory of man in his life. Grayson's daughter represents the opportunity and the need for a caring consciousness-to-consciousness encounter. The reward for opening his consciousness to the encounter with another consciousness is the opportunity to communicate as well as to love and to be loved, an opportunity that only a consciousness can understand. On the other hand, Grayson's corporation represents the manipulation of people for personal advancement and success, the rewards of which are money, the satisfaction of the material needs of his family as well as the envy of others. Grayson's choice is between two self-concepts and their integration into his life. He must decide, not whether to go to the hospital or to the plant, but which of the two conflicting theories of man or personality theories he is to make his own. His dilemma is philosophical and universal; it is not a small family or business decision.

Grayson chose the corporation.

4. A fourth consequence of the ghost-in-a-machine theory of man is the enslavement to roles found among people in all walks of life. As long as man thinks of himself as a thing, he believes the fulfillment of that thing to be found in being some specific role: it may be his manhood or her feminity. His role may be that of a "tough-guy" and gang leader or that of an ever-understanding and receptive uncomplaining therapist. In a field-of-consciousness theory of man, every authentic person must say to himself, "What matters is that I am not my roles and that believing myself to be my roles destroys my potential for living."

A New York sociologist devised a simple exercise with a dual purpose: to tell us first what our actual roles are and then to show us how not to be enslaved by them. You can test yourself as follows: Log a record for one day only of all the roles and games you play during that day. Here is an example, produced by Lorne, a recent college graduate.

> 6:00 A.M. Asleep. Role of dreaming and total relaxation. Complete genuineness. Role of being a baby all over again. Deepest feelings are permitted to emerge.
>
> 7:30 A.M. Go to coffee shop for breakfast. Role of customer. Engage in business transaction and jovial small talk with waitress. My private thoughts are left behind.
>
> 8:00 A.M. Drive to work with Cliff and Mike. We talk about the latest sports scores, cars, office gossip and vacations. I enjoy

the role of male companionship, togetherness, in-group feeling, and brotherhood in the "male-talk" role.

8:30 A.M. I greet my boss. I am now in the role of employee. I try to act to impress him, because I may be in line for promotion. I quickly find my place in the status ladder and in the office organization and attempt to fill that role perfectly. I want to be accepted in that role.

10:05 A.M. I flirt with Lola, the girl in the front office. She doubles as receptionist and telephone operator. I am now in the role of a "male on the make." I say those things which will give me Lola's attention and which will impress her. I show her how masculine, desirable, and considerate I am. I wear masculine clothes, make seductive allusions, and do her favors and express great sympathy and understanding.

12:15 P.M. I meet Mother for lunch. I slip into the role of the immature and whining son. I complain about my teeth, my job, and my apartment. I am a child and not an adult. I get moody and depressed. I am not particularly pleasant to Mother, nor am I interested in pleasing her. I am like a sloppy adolescent coming in for some morning breakfast.

2:25 P.M. We have a fire drill in the office building. I am in charge of evacuating the fifth floor. I now play the role of the captain or the commander, of hero, of leader, the dependable tough guy. I have "leadership" potential.

5:15 P.M. I fight the traffic in a rented car and I slip into the role of primitive "kill or be killed" behavior. I assume the role of a jungle animal, behaving in ways of which I will be ashamed later. I slip into the role of an irresponsible and pure instinct for self-seeking and self-preservation. I mistreat the rented car and ignore pedestrians and other drivers.

6:30 P.M. I go to *The Marina* for dinner. It is a fancy restaurant. I now play the role of the wealthy snob—I demand service and respect. I spend money as if it were water, tipping everyone and ordering the most expensive item on the menu. I fancy myself a wine connoisseur. I play the role of the aristocrat.

11:00 P.M. I go home and to bed, wishing I had Lola in my arms sleeping next to me. I dream of filling the role of a great lover. I return to the reveries of my unconscious, playing no role at all, or again, that of an infant who is prey solely to his instincts and his impulses.

This list is a record of the various roles Lorne plays in one day. If he understands the field-of-consciousness theory of man he knows that while he *plays* all of these roles in truth he *is* none of them. His true self is the consciousness that has, observes, entertains, or chooses these roles—not the roles themselves. The roles are objects to his consciousness; they are organizations of the data or objects of the world and he is in danger of confusing his consciousness with these objects. The roles are things—sociological things; Lorne is not a thing, he is a consciousness. He is free. The roles are his in the same sense that the negative pole of a magnet *is* the positive pole of that magnet.

In the ghost-in-a-machine theory of man, Lorne *is* these roles. He is thus committed to play them out exactly as they are written by the demands of society. He is therefore a slave. If he should ever get used to this slavery, he will have lost the ability to recognize what is human in himself and in others. I believe that if the world continues to subscribe to the ghost-in-a-machine theory of man, the result will be the eventual elimination of man from the face of the earth: not by ecological pollution or nuclear holocaust, but by philosophical misdefinition.

What is the practical point of knowing the difference between Lorne's real self and the roles that this self plays? Knowledge of the difference is freedom from the confusion, freedom from the enslaving consequences of identification. A person who has freed himself from the enslavement of roles can choose and change roles deliberately and rationally. In the case of Lorne, the following happened. As he became free from his slavish identification with and dependency on his roles, he discovered that the role he really wanted was that of a scholar. For him this was the best reflection of the field that is his consciousness, creating a continuity of his inner consciousness with the practical world around him. His scholarship was an *expression* of consciousness onto the world and an incorporation of the world into consciousness. No other role fit his field of consciousness equally well.

He promptly resigned from his job and entered graduate school, specializing in Greek philology. That was a role deliberately and authentically chosen by his conscious inwardness. This authentic choice was possible only by having abandoned the "ghost" theory and having integrated into his manner of existing in the world the field-of-consciousness theory of man. Lorne has not regretted this decision.

5. The individual who has completely integrated the ghost-in-a-machine theory into his life will develop symptoms once the joys of immediate rewards and gratification have passed. He will feel that life is meaningless and that his existence lacks purpose. As a result he will need more and more physical stimulation. If a person thinks he is an object, then he also believes that happiness is to be found in a specific physical sensation. He will turn more and more to titillations: overeating, alcohol, spending money on baubles, taking drugs, sexual perversions, violence—first in fantasy and then in reality. His final physical sensation may be murder or suicide, or both. The escalation is inevitable. We live in a supersaturated culture whose insensitivity

requires an ever-increasing violence of excitement. We have lost the sense of peace and silence and have succumbed to an exponentially growing fever of activity.

The person who knows that he is a field of consciousness will not search invariably for increased physical sensations but will instead be able to rest peacefully and meaningfully in the security of his inward consciousness and the joy that is the meeting of and caring for another consciousness. He will not seek pleasure and property exclusively, but will require primarily meaning and love.

6. The person who thinks he is a thing has no self-confidence; he lacks any sense of genuine independence. He cannot make decisions. He does not understand the meaning of being an individual, because he has no respect for uniqueness in himself and in others. Moreover, he has no base of operations, no home, and no headquarters. He has all the attributes of a thing; he is hard, unfeeling, unloving, unresponsive, and not at peace. Self-confidence and independence are characteristics of consciousness only, never of things or objects. Self-reliance is a trait of a consciousness that is self-conscious, not of a thing that merely exists, is there, vegetates in its concreteness. Security and self-respect are the result of knowing the permanence, primacy, and indestructibility of consciousness. These strengths can never follow from being an object, because every object is finite and ephemeral or, as the theologian would say, contingent. Only consciousness is experienced as a universal phenomenon.

7. The ghost-in-a-machine theory of man leads to imitation rather than creativity. The creative mind is a consciousness at work; it feels and expresses its nature. Consciousness is the act of freedom creating. The notion of creativity makes sense only within a philosophy of consciousness. Creativity as a human value can never be derived from the characteristics of objects, be they organismic or inert. A thing is programmed and replicated; it has no possibility for originality. The artist, the inventor, the original thinker, and the innovator in all walks of life therefore are persons who know they are a *consciousness* and not a *thing*. They have integrated the field-of-consciousness theory of man into their being.

He who believes that he is an object like an animal or a rock will never be able to produce a single original idea—that is, an idea, an act, a work of art, an invention, business, firm, corporation, or an institution which is a novel organization that springs into existence like the universe being created by God, ex nihilo. That is why creativity can never be taught, it can only be uncovered, discovered, and experienced.

8. The ghost-in-a-machine theory of man has no room for freedom. Freedom is our most precious personal possession and most valuable national resource. Freedom is also what makes us human, and if man

is a thing he is not free. If he thinks of himself as a thing, he can have no respect for the institution of freedom in our society. A thing cannot respect the freedom of others because it does not discover freedom in itself. Furthermore, such a man is incapable of using his own freedom. The mark of an authentic society is that it holds freedom sacred above all; and the mark of an authentic man is that he unfailingly acts in accordance with the free nature that he is. He assumes responsibility for his life; he can make choices and decisions. An authentic individual is proud of his freedom because he knows that it is his human essence. Only a field-of-consciousness theory of man allows for the unquestioned existence and the untarnished dignity of human freedom.

To say that man is a thing is to deny his freedom and is thus the death of civilization. A free society will say to its members, "Each of you has the right to develop his life as he individually sees fit." An unfree society will say, "We know what you should become, we know what is good for you and we will force you to live accordingly."

Consider an example. A free man can say, "I have decided to redefine myself from a person who *cannot* handle his problem job to a person who *can*." Greg hated his job as a supervisor in a can manufacturing company. It was an excellent job for an unskilled laborer, but the personal working conditions were completely unacceptable to him. He could not quit because the money was good and he had three children and a pregnant wife to support. An economic recession was in full swing and no other jobs were available. His situation became intolerable. He could not choose to quit nor could he choose to stay. Then he gradually learned the meaning of the fact that he *is* free. His true choice was between (1) "I am a man who *can* handle this conflict" and (2) "I am a man who *cannot* handle this conflict." Up to now, Greg had chosen himself as a man who could not handle the conflict between staying or quitting. He had thought it was a *fact* that he could not handle the conflict. Now he knows he has a *choice*. He knows that there are two types of people: those who can manage life as they find it and those who cannot. He also knows that he chooses his own definition of who he is. Greg has discovered that he had defined himself as a person who could *not* cope with life. He now took personal responsibility for the decision which he tacitly had made and lived, making it relatively easy to change that decision, because he saw that this choice of self-definition was not inevitable.

Fortunately for Greg's wife and children, he chose to redefine himself as a man who *can* handle the conflict, a man who *can* cope with life. Once that decision was accomplished, he was able to make a second choice—he decided to keep his job, put up with it, and advance beyond it.

Within three months Greg was named manager of his division.

Within this chapter we have examined the human consciousness using a number of helpful metaphors. The following statements, representing various existential themes, can now be seen to represent a person who is striving to live by a field-of-consciousness concept of being.

"I am neither a body nor a soul but a continuous consciousness-body-world field."

"I choose myself as one who is realistically flexible."

"I experience time as living in a present which, while utilizing the past, connects directly and primarily into my future."

"My life is an endless process of growing, emerging, and reaching out."

"There exists a consciousness within me which I am and which is eternal."

"I always choose because I am always free."

"As an adult I can choose to meet, confront, witness, understand, and be mirrored by another. I can also choose to love and care for that person."

These themes will be more fully discussed in Chapter 3 within the Master Table. Now, we are ready to discuss two concepts of consciousness that shape our personality and our environment.

2:

Two Concepts
of Consciousness

Our Self-Concept Shapes Our
Personality and Our
Environment

Each of us has two self-concepts or self-images. One is social and the other individual. Our *social* self-image is a cultural affair. The social self-concept is that aspect of our self-image which we all share as members of the human race and as partners in our community. It shapes our civilization, our political institutions, our religious ceremonies, the direction of our scientific and technological progress.

For example, our social self-concept tells us that all men are created equal, and therefore we have a Bill of Rights which we expect the courts to implement. Our social self-concept tells us that progress is good, and therefore the technological revolution is permitted to advance unchecked and destroy the balance of nature as well as economic and social balances. Our social self-concept tells us that pride in our country is right, and therefore we are willing to fight wars. Our social self-concept tells us that advancement and success are values, and therefore we compete rather than cooperate, we seek supremacy rather than compassion. Our social self-concept tells us that human beings are bodies rather than minds, and therefore we come to believe that a loving and caring encounter is achieved by the proper techniques of sexual manipulation.

Furthermore, our social self-concept tells us that we *are* our bodies and that a young body is better than an old body. We accept and introject that idea and submit to much meaningless cosmetic surgery and related operations in the vain hope that visually improving the body will lead to fulfillment in the mind.

Our *individual* self-concept or self-image is, on the other hand, a personal affair. Our individual self-concept is that aspect of ourselves which we do not share with others; it is that part which is exclusively and uniquely ours. Our individual self-image shapes our unique personality and our individualized life-style and not those of the culture and society. An individual self-concept is a program that organizes our individual and private life. Let us consider some examples, primarily of negative self-images.

An individual self-image, learned early in life and at a preconceptual level, may say "I am a failure." The seed that holds this self-image then grows into a total life-style. The individual with that self-image in his program will create situations which cleverly but invariably lead to failure. Janice, for instance, is always willing to take on another assignment—from the PTA, the teacher, her husband, the church membership committee, or the League of Women Voters. She automatically commits herself to tasks that are too numerous and too difficult for her to handle. She makes these commitments, unconsciously, to be sure, in order to assure failure. Her failure program governs her life. That program directs most aspects of her life. We can, as a result, predict her behavior by it.

Another popular individual self-concept is "I am your servant." The perennial servant will never assert himself, will always be timid, will allow himself to be used by others. He will never take his legitimate claims seriously. He does not accept himself and the claims to be himself as real. Walter, ever since he can remember, has had an overwhelming need to be popular. He ascertains what others want, then does it for them and in return expects their gratitude. He wants to please his boss, his wife, his parents, and his teachers. He would make an excellent butler, albeit somewhat demanding of approval. But he forgets throughout to please himself. Everyone likes Walter— but he is soon forgotten and he is certainly ignored if assignments are given out that require a well-developed sense of responsibility and a mature sense of leadership. Walter is the victim of an individual self-concept implanted early into his personality. His health and self-respect require that he change that self-image.

Richard's self-image consists of a different program. It reads "You are attacking me." Richard is therefore always aggressively on the defensive. He is distrustful, hostile, and unpleasant because he responds not to the real person he meets but to the attacker he has invented. He fabricates reasons for his behavior such as "You do not recognize my skill," or "You are not paying adequate attention to me," or "I need no one; I am fully independent." But the true reason for his aggressiveness is in the program of his self-image. As a result of that distorted self-image, Richard makes all those around him miserable and creates an armed camp rather than a loving home as his environment.

Applications

Let us now apply these ideas to the life of you, the reader. How can you tell what your individual self-concept is? There exists a simple but effective procedure. Take a good objective look at your life— perhaps with the help of a trusted friend. Now comes the crucial point. Make the assumption that you brought about your relations with people and your life-style deliberately. Tell yourself "I created my world. I created my personality and I am responsible for my personality. I created my social relations and I am responsible for them. I constructed my environment; I alone am responsible for my environment and only I can change my environment." (This principle will be listed in Chapter 3, which summarizes the consequences of the intentional theory of consciousness in twenty-one themes, as A3.) A general rule is that your individual world—personal, social, and environmental—is a strong clue to your self-image. If you are, let us say, twenty-five years old, you may assume that for at least twenty of those years your self-concept has functioned as a guidance system to direct your perceptions of the world.

After ten years of no philosophical reflection at all, Sally finds herself in a marriage that offers her no opportunity for fulfillment. She is far more educated than Varner, her husband. Furthermore, Sally is dependent, open, and loving—while her husband is closed and independent. In addition Varner is cruel and Sally resents but accepts his inconsiderateness. If Sally now admits to herself that she married Varner precisely so that she could suffer—and it is not only painful but requires strength and courage to make that admission, to integrate that insight into her total life-style—then she will have a clue to the individual self-concept that works within her like a hidden program or secret guidance system. Sally's self-concept is "I must be punished. I must remain forever unfulfilled. I do not deserve a happy life." She may discover that self-concept by deliberately assuming total responsibility for the life she is in fact leading. She is now ready to intelligently eliminate the compulsion to repeat her self-destructive patterns.

In other words, a self-concept functions in the creation of a society and in the development of an individual personality as nucleic acid or a DNA molecule functions in the manufacture and repetition of hereditary characteristics. For example, bacteriophages are viruses that inject their nucleic acid (the very complex DNA double-helix molecule) into bacteria. The bacterium is now no longer able to reproduce itself but instead is programmed to produce large numbers of identical replicas of the original bacteriophage virus. In addition, all plants and animals have their specific characteristics—which are hereditary and thus transmitted from generation to generation—because of the program written into the structure of the complex DNA molecule. The DNA molecule is a tiny gene on a chromosome and it directs and plans the development of the cell—which is vast in size compared to that solitary molecular program—that it inhabits and, eventually, of the total organism of which it is a part.

In like fashion, a social self-concept is a tiny program which is shared (and influenced) by many members of a society, thus creating the structure of that society and affecting individual self-concepts, which themselves are carried like minute gyroscopes within us, directing the path of our bodies and behaviors.

A highly significant principle follows from these considerations. If we wish to control hereditary characteristics, cell multiplication, and the development of the physical characteristics of organisms, we must go to the source cause, the DNA molecule, and make changes there. Similarly, if we wish to improve the quality of our lives, we must discover the self-concept that causes the trouble and exchange it for one that will produce the life that we want and deserve. It is here that philosophy can fulfill its promise of compassion for the suffering of mankind. Because consciousness creates our individual and our world image, consciousness can also change the images, from destructive to constructive ones, from stale ones to creative ones, and from pained to joyous world-views.

Only one of our two self-concepts accurately reflects the structure of consciousness. We now turn to an analysis of that self-image.

The Two Conflicting Self-Concepts

We have now established the fact that the life and world of every individual is controlled by his self-concepts, individual and social. Our culture today is governed by a widespread and dangerous self-concept. If we replace it with a new philosophic one that is healthy and accurate, we can change our individual lives from despair to joy, the life of our society from alienation to brotherhood and make progress in changing from war to peace. Just as a healthy and honest self-concept enables an individual to have a healthy and fulfilled life, the self-concept of a society can influence its behavior.

Let us begin the analysis of the conflict between an authentic and an inauthentic self-concept with an example. Let us look at two entirely different, in fact sharply opposed, opinions on what love—a deep relationship between a man and a woman—really is. Let us contrast love as seen within a distorted conception of consciousness, with love as perceived in the context of what existential phenomenology calls an intentional theory of consciousness, as explained in the previous chapter. Lynn, a recent college graduate and an aspiring young actress who is working in a Los Angeles restaurant-club while taking dancing and acting lessons, writes to me about meeting one of America's most famous actors.

Dear Dr. Koestenbaum:

I had quite an unusual experience last night. Mr. X is a frequent customer in the restaurant I work in. He's —— years old, is extremely intelligent, quite wealthy and has a heart condition that the public knows nothing about and, thus, feels time is rapidly running out. We had a long talk; he wanted to know about me—asked me a lot about myself, informed me that he is nothing *but* honest and because time is an important element, he objects violently to any sort of game-playing. Now, to get to the heart of this, he wants my "company" a couple nights a week—to have conversation etc., and sex would be a part of it—*but* he *emphatically* informed me he would *never force* me to do anything I didn't want—we did *not* have to have intercourse. Wow, he said he realized I needed to get *something* out of a situation like this. He said he would give me a couple hundred dollars a week. He would also help me out anyway he was able to—career-wise.

As I sat there and listened, I was astounded that *I* was listening to all of this and it was happening to me. This man has studied psychology in school and is constantly reading this type of material. I may add he is an avid believer in *Freud*. And, I may add, he has two double sessions with what he called a "shrink"—a week. So he used his "psychological" background on me. He told me if I agreed with this setup I would grow fantastically from the knowledge I could learn from him on life, the Business —and other miscellaneous bullshit.

I felt he was using tricks on me that his psychiatrist uses on him: his trying to reveal something shocking to me about myself. He embarked on an extensive monologue telling me how he could help me overcome my "hangups" or whatever. I said this was not the type of situation in which I would even *attempt* to iron out what problems I *may* have! I restated that I *could not* become sexually involved with him. Then, he pointed out the benefits, again: 1. money, 2. knowledge I could gain, and 3. his helping me become free. Oh yes, he told me I was *not* free. That I was restricting myself.

He then told me there was three hundred dollars in my purse which he had put there when I left the room to go to the ladies room—he thought I would probably agree to his proposition and he didn't like the money end of it—so he secretively put it in my purse.

Before we examine the theory of consciousness implicit in the actor's conception of love, let us ponder the contrasting view of love expressed by the late British philosopher and mathematician, Lord Bertrand Russell. His poem is dedicated to the one who was probably the final beloved in his life and it is found, in the original handwriting, as the frontispiece to the first volume of his *Autobiography*:[1]

To Edith

Through the long years
    I sought peace.
I found ecstasy, I found anguish,
    I found madness,
I found loneliness.
I found the solitary pain
    that gnaws the heart,
But peace I did not find.

Now, old and near my end,
    I have known you,
And, knowing you,
I have found both ecstasy and peace.
    I know rest,
After so many lonely years.
I know what life and love may be—
Now, if I sleep,
I shall sleep fulfilled.

Let us now examine the two personality theories or conceptions of consciousness behind these two expressions of "love."

The episode with X in Lynn's letter is based on the view that happiness consists of manipulating objects, and that human beings are things meant expressly to be used for gratification. Women are sex-things and men are sex-machines. Love is a purchased physical titillation: it is a commodity that can be bought with money, with the allure of advancement, the temptation of widened experience, and the promise of sheer pleasure. The assumption is made that fulfillment and contentment in life can be achieved through this materialistic mode of perception.

When Bertrand Russell speaks of love he speaks from an entirely different space. He refers to human inwardness, to the peaceful conscious center. He refers to values and beauties that can be understood only by a human subjectivity and not by anything developing out of the objective animal organism. He most emphatically does not refer to man the body exclusively, man the thing, the organism,

[1] *The Autobiography of Bertrand Russell* (Boston: Little, Brown and Co., 1951).

the object. He recognizes that the first nature of man is to be a conscious subjectivity, an inward ego. And that ego is pure awareness, pure inwardness, and is not a material object of any kind. This contrasting view of human nature—that the essence of man is first his consciousness and not merely his body—is the field-of-consciousness theory of man, described in the previous chapter. The view that we are a subjective consciousness first and a material body in a natural world second is the *field theory of man* or the *field-of-being theory of man*.

The principal purpose of this chapter is to clarify the distinction between these two conceptions of man, to show the consequences of each and to demonstrate the truth of the field-of-consciousness theory of man.

Our culture is the incarnation of the ghost-in-a-machine theory of man. It has fully integrated into its operations the conviction that man is a thing, that his values are the values of things, and that his goals are the goals of things. The effect of assimilating this materialistic and objectivistic opinion of ourselves into our personal lives and into our society in general amounts to no less than the death of civilization itself. The *man-is-a-thing* theory is at the root of the destruction of all our specifically human values, such as character, integrity, freedom, reason and compassion. The ghost-in-a-machine theory leads to totalitarianism and authoritarianism in both our personal relations and the political institutions of our society. If man is a thing, then violence and tyranny are but the natural manifestations of the desire to rearrange objects (men) for the sake of a superior social order ("happiness"). Disrespect for inwardness is the badge of the tyrant and the license of the bureaucrat.

On the personal level, the "ghost" theory of man, when applied to daily living, can express itself, especially at the onset of middle age, in the symptom of ennui and a sense of meaninglessness. The same malaise can afflict a society; it is afflicting the United States at this time. We are a society at middle age, incapable of handling the philosophic problem of meaninglessness. We seek additional technology when what we need is deeper understanding of ourselves.

If an engine needs new pistons, the broken ones are discarded and new ones installed in their place. What matters to the mechanic is not the fate of the broken pistons but the success of the engine. If we believe man is a thing then we treat him like a piston. When his needs interfere with the smooth operation of society we discard him to jail or hospital because what matters is the progress of society and not the rights of the individual. And the idea of "rights" makes no sense to one who thinks man is an object or a thing. The concept of "rights" can be understood only in the framework of a field-of-consciousness theory of man.

In the last analysis, the ghost-in-a-machine theory of man could ultimately force us to condone the destruction of crippled children and the infirm aged because their utility to society has ceased. Only the philosophical recognition that each man possesses—or *is*—a conscious inwardness can save individuals from inconsiderateness and indifference and our society from the barbarism toward which it is headed.

The mechanization of man is perhaps most dangerous in that noble profession, medicine. Yet the pervasive influence of the ghost-in-a-machine theory in that discipline is often almost beyond belief. Gerry, a Ph.D. in biophysics and molecular biology from one of the nation's most prestigious universities, was working for his second doctorate, in psychiatry, when he wrote to me:

> I am presently studying in almost total seclusion for the Medical College Admission Test I am required to take in two weeks. It involves mostly refreshing my memory with all the intricate details of general biology, chemistry, and physics, as well as little-used English vocabulary. Questions on existential philosophy, phenomenology, or even just meaningful questions in humanistic areas are certainly not represented on this test that examines the preparation of our future doctors. Instead they ask questions such as which of four obscure reagents is best for separating cadmium from copper ions or what number the product of the specific heat and atomic weight is for metals.

Philosophy leads to health (in persons and in society) because it changes our views from a ghost-in-a-machine theory to a field-of-consciousness theory of man and because that change in self-concept leads to a new man, to new relations among people and a new social order.

Examples

Many Americans saw a dreadful and terrifying NBC television program on July 28, 1972. It was an hour-long interview with two Utah convicts: Walter Kelbach and Myron Lance. These two men recounted how together and in a brief span of time they knifed and shot to death six people. They represent the ultimate in the degeneration that follows from refusing to recognize and be sensitive to the subjective, conscious inwardness of other human beings.

The essentials that the interview disclosed about the criminals were these:

1. They were sane, legally and psychiatrically. Two psychologists testified to that.

2. They were on pills and beer but nevertheless aware of what they were doing. The drugs facilitated the acting out of their impulses and fantasies. They *wanted* to kill. They took the drugs voluntarily, to help themselves do what they wanted to do.

3. The murder spree was a joyful experience. They delighted in terrifying, killing, shooting, and knifing innocent victims and were amused by their success in evading the police.

4. In recounting the crimes, they found great humor in some of the horror situations they created and in their victims' panic, bargaining, and prayers. Sadism was part of their joy; a typical comment was made by Lance as he recalled his knifing of a gas station attendant: "He was gagging on his blood, and it just hit me kind of funny. So I got him with the knife and he quit his gagging."

5. The lifelong possession and use of knife and gun gave them a sense of power, worth, dignity, respectability, and significance. The world recognized their existence and the weapons gave them enormous freedom of movement (space and time) in the world.

6. They enjoyed greatly the newspaper and television publicity.

7. Their background, family and personal, was one of total violence.

8. They experienced no remorse, regret, or pity for any of their victims nor for the orphans that they created.

The crucial point is the final item—the inability to feel pity for their victims. If a man has the capacity for empathy and pity he will refrain from crime.

What is missing in a person who lacks a sense of compassion? The answer is simple—compassion is possible only if we know that man is a conscious inwardness, a subjective center, an experiencing ego, and not just a body or a mass of protoplasm that is disposable and replaceable. One source of the criminal mentality is total ignorance of the conscious nature of any and every man. If he has a clear knowledge and perception of the inwardness of his potential victims, then it will not be easy for him to hurt them. In failing to recognize the consciousness of his victim, the criminal also fails to perceive the existence of his own consciousness. Kelbach and Lance were not mentally ill—they were philosophically ignorant. And our society today is in danger of a similar gross ignorance!

There are basically only three explanations for criminal acts: insanity (i.e., perceptual and conceptual distortion of reality), philosophical ignorance, or deliberate and free choice. The two men in question were sane. Their crimes are therefore due either to gross philosophical ignorance—that is, ignorance about the structure of the field of consciousness, ignorance about the existence of human subjectivity and of its holy nature—or they are due to a deliberate choice of denying the mandate and claims of that philosophical insight. They are thus either ignorant or evil. If they are ignorant they must be taught and if they are evil they must be punished. However, the expression "must be taught" refers to more than mere verbal repetition; it means integration into the personality. By the time middle age is reached, reteaching in this sense may well be impossible. I hope not, and I have chosen to live and act on that hope.

The controversial book and film *A Clockwork Orange* describes a society in which both criminals and the Establishment reflect the thorough application of the ghost-in-a-machine theory of man. Criminals and ministers of justice, murderers and law-enforcement officers become indistinguishable. And the cure for crime in *Clockwork Orange,* as in any society based on this theory, is reconditioning. The reconditioned and "rehabilitated" felon has not lost his free will. What has happened to him is that whenever the sexual and criminal urges surface in him his body becomes violently ill. His subjectivity has not been affected; but his options for action have been severely limited. His body has been modified. After behavior modification, the criminal, being human, is subjectively as free as he was before. The difference now is that he is jailed—not behind prison bars but inside his reconditioned body.

3:

The Master Outline

The Master Table, which is both a theoretical summary and a practical test, is a highly efficient teaching device. It is an exercise. It is conceptual, but it also is experiential.

The Master Table is a carefully constructed, brief, and formalized statement of those aspects of our human existence which need to be known and applied in order to lead an authentic life. The scores on the test exercise associated with it are of course in no way as important as the activity. By taking the test exercise, you will be compelled to think about the basics of the existential personality theory. Also, by comparing your own life to these existential ideals, you will become aware of the extent to which you think that you are a mature and authentic individual. New perspectives on life may be opened in this manner.

Each theme in the test exercise consists of five parts. First, you will find a succinct expression or a simple word that characterizes a particular theme of the existential personality theory. (For example, theme A2 is called "The Two Selves.") Second, you are given a sentence that has been carefully constructed to summarize a considerable amount of existential research into the nature of man and thus to present an ideal human condition as well. An example would be C9, which is explained and developed in these words: "I am free to make commitments." Third, you will find enclosed in parentheses the technical term associated with the theme in question, as in B1: "Phenomenology." That is included for those professionally interested in philosophy.[1] Fourth, you will find, also in parentheses, an explanatory paragraph discussing in reasonably simple and nontechnical language the philosophic meaning of each one of these themes. Finally,

---

[1] The technical terms are here for reference only. A fuller theoretical foundation for the existential personality theory and its relation to both philosophy and science is found in my book *The Vitality of Death: Essays in Existential Psychology and Philosophy* (Westport, Conn.: Greenwood Press, 1971). I refer the interested reader to that book.

also in parentheses, you will find the abbreviation for that theme as it is used on the profile (such as Li for Life).

You will also notice that the test exercise is divided into three main sections: The *nature, rule,* and *principles* of human existence. These three categories correspond roughly to the three fields studied in an existential phenomenology. The nature of human existence is an elaboration of the general metaphysical or so-called ontological characteristics of an intentional consciousness. The themes discussed under category A describe the fundamental aspects of being or of reality as experienced and conceptualized by what is my idea of an existential phenomenology.

The theme discussed under B refers to the emphasis on methodology that is typical of an existential phenomenology. The method of acquiring truth is descriptive rather than logical, experiential rather than inferential or deductive. The method is in the spirit of science, in that phenomenology demands unprejudiced and assumption-free observations to serve as the basis for any theories about man.

Finally, the themes discussed under C are what I call existentialism proper; that is, daily rules—ethical or practical, therapeutic or pragmatic—to guide us toward fulfillment and to help us cope with the various problems of human existence.

Rate Yourself and Check
Your Progress

Use the Master Table as a subjective evaluation of the extent to which you understand and use an existential philosophy in your life. Take this test exercise twice, once before and once after you finish this book and have had a chance to reflect on its contents. The significance of your score lies not in its absolute value but in the change that occurs from the first to the second time, or any other time, you perform the test exercise. It is also interesting and insightful for you to examine the relation between your understanding or conceptual ideals and your opinion on how you use that understanding. An extended explanation of your score is discussed in the next chapter, which analyzes the meaning of the profile.

Instructions

Answer the following two questions about each of the nineteen (19) themes of the Master Table. Be slow, careful and thoughtful. Plan to spend approximately one and one-half hours on the test exercise and feel free to pause occasionally.

Question I. "*To what extent do I agree intellectually with the idea, statement or concept?*" Choose your answers from among the following alternatives:

0.   I do not understand the idea.
10. I do *not* agree *at all.*
20. I agree *very little.*
30. I agree to a *reasonable* extent.
40. I agree *very much.*
50. I agree *almost completely.*
60. I agree *totally, enthusiastically* and *without reservations.*

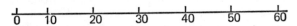

Question II. "*How often do I use this idea, statement, or concept in my life? How often do I find that this idea is integrated into my style of life? How accurately does the concept describe me as I truly am?*" Choose your answers from among the following alternatives:

0.   Since I do not understand the idea, I do not know if I apply it.
10. I *never* apply it. I *never* am like that.
20. I *rarely* apply it. I *rarely* am like that.
30. I *occasionally* apply it. I *occasionally* am like that.
40. I *frequently* apply it. I *frequently* am like that.
50. I apply it *most of the time.* I am like that *most of the time.*
60. I apply it *always* and *enthusiastically.* I am like that *always* and *enthusiastically.*

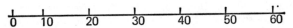

Answer according to the following directions: Mark an X in the appropriate place of the scale. After you have made all your marks, translate each mark into a number. For example

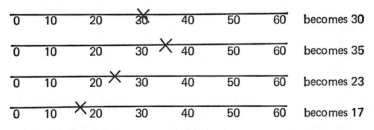

Use the answer sheets that appear at the end of the Master Table.

The Master Table

The following master outline summarizes the insights about the nature of man and the character of his happiness developed by a hundred years of existential philosophy. The outline is carefully formulated to emphasize the practical application of existential philosophy.

Read the list carefully. The subsequent discussion and case histories will explain the meanings of these insights.

A. The *Nature* of Human Existence (Metaphysics, Ontology)
   1. The Field Theory of Man. "I am neither a body nor a soul but a continuous consciousness-body-world field." (Intentionality)

Explanation: I do not exist in isolation. I am one with other people and one with nature. Whatever affects other people and the environment also affects me, and whatever happens to me affects other people and the world around me. (FT)

   2. The Two Selves. "I am a pure consciousness that has a psychological personality, a physical body, and many social roles." (Transcendental and empirical egos)

Explanation: I am more than just a body and even more than a personality. I am also a pure consciousness or a pure awareness that is different from the person that is known by the name that I carry and the likeness that I am. I am a center, the depths of which only I can plumb (TS).

   2a. Four Modes of Consciousness. "Consciousness can be experienced as either individual, intimate, cosmic, or as an Eternal Now." (Transcendental intersubjectivity)

Explanation: I understand that there is much confusion about the nature of the ego, because different cultures have different definitions of what it means to be a self. I am capable and willing to experience and identify with at least four separate and increasingly deeper and more universal ways in which the consciousness that I am or that runs through me can manifest itself in me.

The first, and most common, is the experience of consciousness as being an individual. Individual consciousness is the silent and solitary center of all my experiences. Individual consciousness feels comfortable with itself but isolated from other people and from the world of nature.

I am also an intimate or intersubjective consciousness. I can experience complete oneness with another person. There exists a perceptible connecting conscious space between me and another person. I can perceive the center of another person directly; I can also sense how another experiences my center directly.

Third, I can experience the fact that I am part of a cosmic conscious stream and that I share and participate fully in the endless processes of nature. I am a wave in an ocean of consciousness; I am a well, as all others are wells (to use Ira Progoff's metaphor) which taps into a single underground stream, together with all the other wells. I am coterminous with empty space-time.

A fourth, final, and the deepest level in which consciousness manifests itself is what can be called the Eternal Now. In it, even space-time becomes an object to consciousness. The Eternal Now as the source of consciousness is experienced to be outside of space and time. A psychic distance has been inserted between the ego as the Eternal Now and its most primitive objects, empty space and time (MC).

3. Responsibility. "I have created and am responsible for the organization of my world. I did not create the raw materials, but I am fully and alone responsible for the social reality that I have constructed around me and the life-style that I have organized for myself." (Constitution)

Explanation: If I am happy and successful, then it is essentially not fate and luck but my own efforts and decisions that have led to my well-being. If I fail and am unhappy, then I am prepared to assume full responsibility for my problems. I feel that my problems are basically my fault because I am in charge of my life—no one else is. It is good news to know that I help shape both the good and the bad in the world in which I live. I am prepared to fulfill my obligations. (Rs)

B. The *Rule* for a Meaningful Human Existence (Methodology)
    1. Self-disclosure. "I must be fully disclosed to myself both as a human being and as ——— (write your name in this space)." (Phenomenology)

Explanation: I am excited at the thought of both therapy and philosophy. I look forward to exploring the person that I am. I anticipate with pleasure examining my feelings and attitudes. I want to study my personality and my body. I am also determined to understand the philosophical nature of man. I recognize the importance of questions regarding human destiny and about the meaning of life. I also appreciate the significance of morality. I consider these questions fundamental to a free and healthy life. (SD)

C. The Sixteen *Principles* for Authentic Human Existence (Philosophical Anthropology)

1. Pain. "*I choose to value my pains.*" (*Negation, Anxiety*)

Explanation: Suffering can be a learning experience. Pain is unavoidable. Death is a natural part of life. Anxiety and depression help me understand the meaning of life. I can successfully cope with the fact that evil is an integral part of life. (P)

2. Death. "*I choose to value my limitations.*" (*Negation, Finitude*)

Explanation: I can adapt myself to frustrations. I know that much of the time I cannot have what I want. I know that over a lifetime I will be forced to give up many of my most cherished dreams. I am successful in accepting that which cannot be helped. I can accept the fact that all life ends in death. (D)

3. Reflection. "*I am able both to* live *my life and to* reflect *on my life.*" (*Epoché, Reduction*)

Explanation: There are times when I am active and extraverted. I participate in life and I am involved. There are also times at which I am withdrawn and reflective—that is, introverted. If I so choose, I can meditate and be happy just being by myself and inside myself. I have control over these feelings and attitudes. They are usually appropriate to the circumstances of my life. (Rf)

4. Self-reliance. "*I am an adult consciousness that exists alone: I choose to be independent and self-reliant.*" (*Inwardness, Subjectivity*)

Explanation: I have outgrown childish forms of dependency. I can be comfortable being alone. I can go through life on my own two feet. I can take care of myself—and of others if necessary. I feel that this independence and self-reliance is an attitude that I voluntarily choose and not one that is imposed upon me from the outside. This theme is in contrast to the later themes of commitment (9) and love (10). (SR)

5. Individuality. "*It is right and normal for me to seem different from other human beings.*" (*Uniqueness*)

Explanation: I am free to conform or not to conform as my value system dictates. I am not excessively bothered by the fact that I may be different from my peers. I am prepared to create my own direction and my own life, one that I know is right for me even though it may differ from the prevailing life-styles of those around me. I am not easily pressured by my associates and relatives. Neither am I easily pressured by my neighbors, by people that I meet or by those who try to sell me something. (I)

6. Eternity. "There exists a consciousness within me which I am and which is eternal." (Transcendental ego)

Explanation: This point is perhaps the most difficult one to understand. It means that I have a genuine conception and perception of my most inner inwardness. I have a real sense of the center that I am within me amidst the storms, stresses, and changes of life. I understand what wise men of all ages mean when they refer to the pure consciousness within me that I am. I also recognize the universality of that center. The conscious center that I am is not susceptible to the flux of life and is therefore unchanging and timeless. It may not last forever, but it is outside of time. (E)

6a. Reverence. "Each individual human inward subjectivity is the divine consciousness in man." (Transcendental subjectivity)

Explanation: Reverence for subjectivity is the highest existential principle of morality. A person's character may be evil and his body diseased, but his pure inner conscious core is infinitely precious and eternally dignified. Man's inwardness is the source of his value; his inmost center is the foundation for his "unalienable rights of life, liberty, and the pursuit of happiness" with which each individual, according to the American Declaration of Independence, is born.

I am capable of respecting infinitely the inner ego of both myself and of others. I can "hate the sin rather than the sinner." I agree with Maritain when he says "the true connection among people is spiritual." (Rv)

7. Freedom. "I always choose because I am always free." (Freedom)

Explanation: I have a realistic sense of the profound meaning of human freedom. I believe in the existence of free will. I believe that I am responsible for my actions and for my life. I believe that I set my own values and self-concepts and I am prepared to accept the full consequences. I am able to make decisions even while I realize that in most situations there are no definite truths and falsehoods, rights and wrongs. (F)

8. Life. "My first and last choice is to say 'yes' to life." (Affirmation)

Explanation: If I say "yes" to life I recognize that I am fully responsible for whatever optimism or pessimism runs through my existence. If I am depressed *I* have said "no" to life. If I live with joy it is because *I* have said "yes" to life. If I say "yes" to life I freely choose to make living itself the highest value. In short, whether I love life or not, whether I am a positive or a negative personality is my own free personal choice for which I am fully responsible. I cannot blame others for my depression, anger, guilt or lack of self-respect. (Li)

9. Commitment. "I am free to make commitments." (Commitment, cathexis)

Explanation: Commitment and love represent a contrast to the theme of self-reliance (4). Commitment means that I feel connected with the world—I feel one with my body and one with the society and environment into which as a human being I am born. Commitment means that I can risk attachments to people, principles, goals, and life-styles. I can take it if I lose. Commitment means that I can live as a full-fledged participant in the affairs of society and of the natural environment. My life is experienced whole rather than fragmented. (Cm)

9a. Reality. "I clearly distinguish reality from fantasies, dreams, rationalizations and wishful thinking. I am always in touch with what is real." (Ego-cogito-cogitatum)

Explanation: I have a well-developed sense of reality. Even though I understand that the distinction between dream and reality is philosophically ambiguous, I find no difficulty separating dream from reality in my daily and practical life. I know that there is a reality beyond my inwardness. I know that this reality is different from my subjective ego. I know that this reality may be other people or the objects of nature, but it can also be my body or my unconscious (as I see in cases of physical or mental illness). I know that this reality is independent of me: sometimes it joins me in my needs and wishes, sometimes it is indifferent and sometimes it opposes me. Nevertheless, at all times I feel that I am directly in touch with that external reality. I always sense that I am in contact with that part of the world which is other than me. Even while I am rationalizing, deceiving myself, or having fantasies, I know that what is real is that I am dreaming. (Rl)

10. Love. "As an adult I can choose to meet, confront, witness, understand, and be mirrored by another. I can also choose to love him and care for him." (Encounter)

Explanation: I am capable of loving like an adult. I can love spiritually and I can love physically. I do not use love neurotically. In love I can accept the dignity and the needs of my partner in love. If I so choose, I am able to make love the central project in my life. I enjoy spiritual, emotional and physical love and love is easy and natural for me. (Lv)

11. Adaptability. "I choose myself as one who is realistically flexible." (Flexibility)

Explanation: I can be reflective and inward or active and outgoing, depending on my own choices and the circumstances in which I find myself. I can be self-reliant and independent if I want to and have to, but I also can be dependent and trusting if I choose that personality structure. I can be both a leader and a follower, as my decisions and the world's circumstances dictate. (A)

12. Time. "*I experience time as living in a present which, while utilizing the past, connects directly and primarily into my future.*" (*Futurity*)

Explanation: I experience my life as a continuous progression. My sense of time is not fragmented. My focus is on the future. I live in the present and I realize that both past and future are connected to me in the present. The burdens of the past exist for me in the present. The hopes and opportunities for the future exist for me in the present. I experience the time of my life as a river that flows always and smoothly in the direction of the future. (T)

13. Growth. "*My life is an endless process of growing, emerging and reaching out.*" (*Self-transcendence*)

Explanation: For me, to live is to grow. I am not satisfied with achievements in life. My concern is rather with process and movement in my life. The meaning of my life is found in continual growth—in education, in human relationships, in occupational progress, in creativity, in building, and so forth. I feel that if my growing should end so would the meaning of my life. I know that either hate or disinterest are the results of a reaching out that has been frustrated. (G)

14. Contradiction. "*The inescapable ambiguities and contradictions of life are my powerful allies.*" (*Polarity, Dialectic*)

Explanation: When faced with contradictions in life I am not upset; instead, I am challenged. I realize that values and situations are usually ambiguous and unclear. There are many sides to most issues. I feel no compulsion to discover always the absolute right. I can act in spite of uncertainty. I can make decisions in spite of ambiguities. I can make commitments without being certain of the truth. I can tolerate disagreement, opposition, rejection, and denial. In fact, contradictions are to me a source of strength, because I find polarities within myself. I can integrate the polar opposites in me and achieve a mature sense of wholeness. (Cd)

ANSWER SHEETS

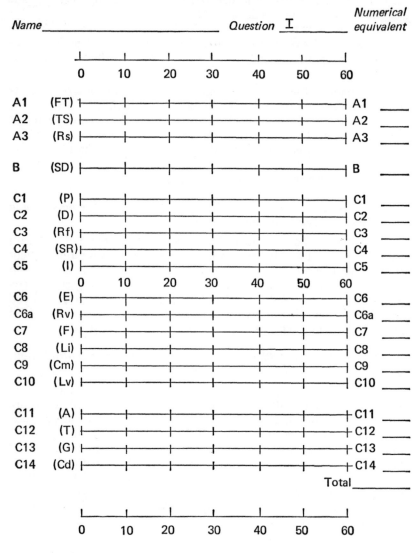

Name_____ Question I_____ *Numerical equivalent*

A1	(FT)	A1 ____
A2	(TS)	A2 ____
A3	(Rs)	A3 ____
B	(SD)	B ____
C1	(P)	C1 ____
C2	(D)	C2 ____
C3	(Rf)	C3 ____
C4	(SR)	C4 ____
C5	(I)	C5 ____
C6	(E)	C6 ____
C6a	(Rv)	C6a ____
C7	(F)	C7 ____
C8	(Li)	C8 ____
C9	(Cm)	C9 ____
C10	(Lv)	C10 ____
C11	(A)	C11 ____
C12	(T)	C12 ____
C13	(G)	C13 ____
C14	(Cd)	C14 ____

Total_____

A2a   (MC)
C9a   (RI)   (Statistics not available for these two scales)

ANSWER SHEETS

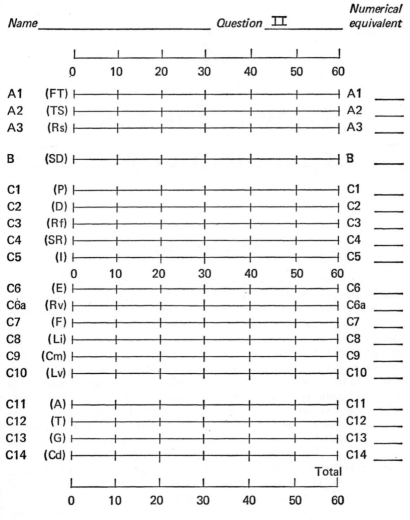

Name_____ Question ⅠⅠ_____ Numerical equivalent

		0	10	20	30	40	50	60		
A1	(FT)								A1	____
A2	(TS)								A2	____
A3	(Rs)								A3	____
B	(SD)								B	____
C1	(P)								C1	____
C2	(D)								C2	____
C3	(Rf)								C3	____
C4	(SR)								C4	____
C5	(I)								C5	____
C6	(E)								C6	____
C6a	(Rv)								C6a	____
C7	(F)								C7	____
C8	(Li)								C8	____
C9	(Cm)								C9	____
C10	(Lv)								C10	____
C11	(A)								C11	____
C12	(T)								C12	____
C13	(G)								C13	____
C14	(Cd)								C14	____

Total

0   10   20   30   40   50   60

A2a (MC)
C9a (RI)   (Statistics not available for these two scales)

4:

How to Interpret
Your Authenticity Profile

Plotting Your Profile

It is now time for you to plot your scores on the profile sheet. You should use one of the authenticity profile blanks that are provided. Follow the directions below in order to develop your authenticity profile. Transfer your numerical score for each of the nineteen existential themes to the appropriate point on the profile. In plotting your graph be sure to note that items (or scales) A 2a and C 9a are not on the profile blank. Because these themes were added late, no statistics for them exist. You must exercise caution: the vertical interval between numbers is not the same from scale to scale; it is therefore necessary to interpolate approximately. For example, the numerical interval from average to above average on the FT scale (Question I) is from 43 to 56, so, this distance is represented by 13 points. A score of 49 or 50, for instance, would then be plotted halfway between average and above average. However, on the E scale, the corresponding distance is represented by 20 points. Also, the order of the scales on the profile is not the same as in the test, so after C 2 you will find C 14 rather than C 3.

When all the dots are in place, connect them to get a graph, as you will see in the samples.

The numbers that you use to plot your answers to Q I appear *above* the horizontal lines, whereas the numbers needed to plot the answers to Q II appear *below* these same horizontal lines. In this manner, maximum information can be incorporated in one profile sheet.

The vertical bars on the left of the profile sheet should be filled in to the level of the *totals* corresponding, respectively, to your answers to Q I, Q II, and to the difference between them. You might wish to consult the sample profiles included in order to gain further clarification.

What can be accomplished with these profiles? We get a better look at the inside of a human being: he does and his counselor does. From then on we proceed intuitively, in the spirit of "Let's talk together about how the world looks to you from your vantage point." Following are guidelines to help bring about that result.

A minor warning is in order. The discussion of profile interpretation may be slightly more esoteric than the other material in this book. To take the Master Table test exercise is a significant value in itself. To interpret it in accordance with the principles discussed in the next sections is not necessary.

The Profile

First, let me make a few observations about the profile in general.

Between the T-scores of 40 and 60 fall some 68 percent of those charted. Fourteen percent of the population falls between the T-scores of 60 and 70, and 14 percent between the T-scores of 30 and 40. Above 70 you find the upper 2 percent of the population—which for this test does not have any statistical meaning—and below 30, the bottom 2 percent.

The table is divided into three major sections: the summary section, the world-view section, and the anthropology section. The summary section provides an overview of the data. The world-view section deals with ontology and methodology. It is related to the general world-view of existentialism. The last section concerns itself with man's being-in-the-world; we might say that it deals with his emotional existence.

You must remember the *tentative character* of the profile. It is true that most subjects who take this test are very serious about their work. They seem to reflect thoughtfully on their answers and try to think of examples before deciding on a response. And it is rather common for subjects to spend two hours on the test. Nevertheless, *there is only one item*, one question, for each philosophic theme. That is not enough of a sample to yield statistically significant measures for your answer. But it is enough to stimulate seriously your thinking about your own authenticity. You must also keep in mind that the standard for this test was developed from reasonably sophisticated adults enrolled in evening philosophy classes or in upper-division university courses. Standards for the general population are not available, but would perhaps be quite different.

What Does Your Profile
Tell You?

You must always remember that this is a test using strictly and exclusively the phenomenological method. It is thus a totally subjective test, a subjective measure of your subjectivity. It is not an objective, behavioral test. Like a mirror, it reflects to you and to others a picture of how it feels to be you. It shows you what it is like to be inside you, how the world looks from the inside of you. The test does that by comparing your subjective feelings with parallel intuitions of others. The test is an attempt to come as close as possible to the incredibly difficult task of comparing subjective intuitions.

The method of phenomenology encourages such subjective explorations. You must live with yourself and you must live your own life. From the point of view of existential authenticity it is not as important to compare yourself to external standards or to the visible behavior of others as it is to understand your own inwardness.

The profile shows how philosophy can be used to help you understand yourself, to help you perceive yourself with increased sensitivity. It shows you how to use existential concepts and values for the sake of comprehending who you are.

What to Look For

The first examples discussed are profiles in which only the answers to Q II are plotted. The meaning of Q I will be considered later.

In order to interpret the meaning of your profile, you must be alert to the following features.

1. Examine its general pattern. Is it high or low? Consistent or inconsistent? Jane's profile is both high and consistent. Anything much higher than that might be artificial—that is, not answered openly and honestly. Mahlon's profile tends to be low and inconsistent. It has high and low points scattered throughout. In addition, it has high and low points in each of the subcategories or areas, especially encounter and survival.

2. Examine each individual area. Ask yourself, "Is it high?" "Is it low?" "Is it consistent?" and "How does it compare to other areas?" If the score in an area is high it would indicate a strength, an asset, in that area. For example, Jane is strong in accepting and integrating the negativities of life (suffering). Mahlon is somewhat weak in the area of free will, and Marilyn tends to be weak in the area of inwardness. Mark, who is strong in the areas of survival, free will, and suffering, can use

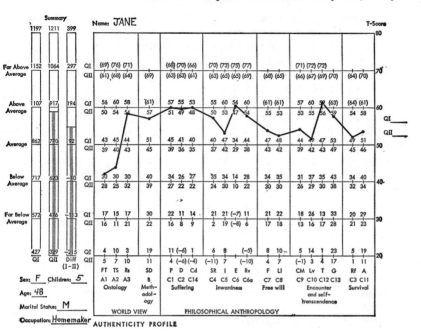

AUTHENTICITY PROFILE

Name: MARILYN

T-Score

Summary
1197 1211 399

Far Above Average	1152	1064	297
Above Average	1107	917	194
Average	862	770	92
Below Average	717	623	−10
Far Below Average	572	476	−113
	427	329	−215
	QI	QII	Diff (I−II)

Sex: F Children: 0
Age: 25
Marital Status: M
Occupation: Teacher

FT TS Rs — A1 A2 A3 — Ontology
SD — B — Methodology
P D Cd — C1 C2 C14 — Suffering
SR I E Rv — C4 C5 C6 C6a — Inwardness
F Li — C7 C8 — Free will
CM Lv T G — C9 C10 C12 C13 — Encounter and self-transcendence
RF A — C3 C11 — Survival

WORLD VIEW PHILOSOPHICAL ANTHROPOLOGY

AUTHENTICITY PROFILE

Name: MARK

T-Score

Summary
1197 1211 399

Far Above Average	1152	1064	297
Above Average	1107	917	194
Average	862	770	92
Below Average	717	623	−10
Far Below Average	572	476	−113
	427	329	−215
	QI	QII	Diff (I−II)

Sex: M Children: 5
Age: 51
Marital Status: M
Occupation: Physician

FT TS Rs — A1 A2 A3 — Ontology
SD — B — Methodology
P D Cd — C1 C2 C14 — Suffering
SR I E Rv — C4 C5 C6 C6a — Inwardness
F Li — C7 C8 — Free will
CM Lv T G — C9 C10 C12 C13 — Encounter and self-transcendence
RF A — C3 C11 — Survival

WORLD VIEW PHILOSOPHICAL ANTHROPOLOGY

AUTHENTICITY PROFILE

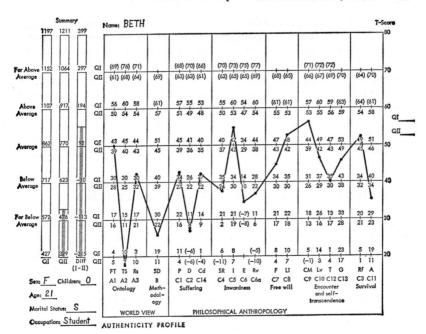

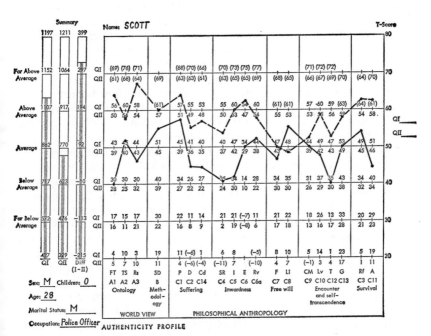

those strengths to enhance his encounter and self-disclosure (he is low in both of these areas). Marilyn, who is strong in ontology and methodology, has an existential outlook on life. That strength can be the foundation for raising her low self-respect (as shown by her low inwardness score). She has an even and high score in ontology and methodology but a saltatory score in the anthropology section. I repeat that a note of caution is in order: You must be wary of excessively high scores. In this test that would mean most scores just under a T-score of 70. The possibility always suggests itself that high scores are intellectual, defensive, and artificial. That is a suspicion worth exploring further.

3. Examine the Q II and Difference scores. The Difference score can be interpreted variously as follows. A low score can mean self-satisfaction, a relaxed and unambitious personality. It can also mean stiffness, repression, and blindness about oneself. In general, a low Difference score seems to indicate a closed mind. It means the individual will not continue to grow. It also means a condition of hopelessness. A high score can mean motivation for self-development, the existence of meanings and goals in life. It can also mean guilt and a sense of inadequacy. In general, a high score means that the individual is open and eager for personalized philosophic work. He has hope.

Let us examine the question, "Do you perceive yourself as an authentic person?" Jane clearly does. Her Q II score is above average. Her Difference score is above average notwithstanding the fact that Q II is high already. The large difference between the conception of her ideal (Q I) and the perception of her actual life or being-in-the-world (Q II) does not come through to her as despair or guilt but as challenge, as the task that is giving meaning to her life.

Beth does not perceive herself as authentic. That can be seen in her extremely low Q II score. In her case, the large Difference score is probably experienced by her as guilt and shame and is thus likely to come across as more of a burden than an incentive.

4. Examine the SD score. You are really answering the following kind of question: "Do you use the phenomenological method, the method of careful and sensitive, assumption-free, and introspective descriptions, in the emotional and feeling aspects of your life?" A low SD score may mean repression or lack of commitment to the task of a personalized philosophy, a philosophy of life, or a philosophy of man. It may mean that this task is unnecessary or irrelevant to the subject. On the other hand, a high score on that item may mean serious commitment to a lived philosophy. The score is only one response to one question; it is nevertheless significant. Even a low score is meaningful, because it was produced by an individual who, with considerable self-sacrifice, has enrolled in a course or a workshop and made a commitment to an arduous program of just the kind of philosophic self-development indi-

cated by that question. He has with that commitment expressed his seriousness about the project of self-disclosure. A low score would still indicate serious and above-average commitment to philosophic and personal self-disclosure, at least in relation to the rest of the population.

5. Study your ontology score. How close to the existential model is your living world-view? How close are you to integrating an existential life-style into your personal world? Marilyn is strongest in this area, even stronger than Jane—who may be the most authentic of the sample group. Marilyn's basic philosophic authenticity—undeveloped up to now—is further confirmed by her high time (T) score. A sense for the unity of time parallels an accurate perception of the structure of consciousness that is central to the field-of-consciousness theory of man. One is tempted to diagnose Marilyn as healthy and strong, but somewhat underdeveloped. Beth, on the other hand, seems to have difficulty with the notion of pure consciousness or the transcendental ego—which is the source of values and strengths. If true, this lacuna would weaken all other aspects of her personality. A good course in existential philosophy may be an excellent prescription for Beth.

6. Study other individual area scores. For example, what is your capacity to manage suffering? In our illustrations, only Mark and Jane have demonstrated that they possess this all-important quality. Beth, the youngest of the group, has the most trouble with that area of her personality.

7. Look for clues. The test can provide clues on how to work most efficiently toward a more authentic human existence. For example, Marilyn scores very low in the inwardness area of her profile; however, she scores surprisingly high on the reverence (Rv) item. It is of course quite possible that her Rv score reflects a purely intellectual rather than an experienced score, whereas her other scores in the inwardness area (SR, I, E) may be emotional and feeling in origin. Even so, that would be of little consequence in prescribing for her an individual program to achieve authenticity. She—or her friend, counselor, teacher, or therapist—must explore the role of the theme of reverence (for herself as well as for others) in her life. It is a strength on which she can build. If the capacity and willingness for reverence is one of her personality assets, she can use it as a clue to lift and build up her sagging self-confidence, independence, and self-respect.

Beth is also low in the inwardness area. She can raise her sense of inner strength, her maturity and feelings of personal solidity by exploring what is behind her relatively high individuality (I) score. She will find a living asset on which and with which she can build.

8. Watch for very high scores. As was suggested earlier, exceedingly high T-scores must be approached cautiously. More likely than not they are an exaggeration and may indicate the exact opposite of what they

appear to be on the surface. For example, look at the high score for D on Mark's profile. On the one hand, his high D score, together with the other high scores in the area of suffering, may be an index of strength and stoic acceptance of the negative realities of life. However, the exaggerated score on D, when compared to a low degree of hope as indicated by a low Difference score, might have quite different and more dramatic meanings. To Mark, the virtue of death may be that it is the only hope in a totally hopeless life. Mark may be out-and-out suicidal. Death is then accepted as a beautiful way out of a life that has lost all meaning. This direction of questioning is worth pursuing in the case of Mark.

Individual Profiles

We are now ready for a closer look at our sample profiles.

Outstanding in Mark's profile is his survival power. Also, his low score on TS may be related to his physiologically oriented medical outlook on life. He may be disinclined to make room for the concept of pure consciousness because the emphasis in medicine is on the body as the truly human part of ourselves. One consequence of a low TS score is perhaps his equally low Rv score. If there is no inward consciousness, then there is nothing to revere either. The high suffering and low Rv and Rs scores suggest an ethical but nonreligious man. Similarly, a high score on the Rs-E-Rv constellation—all of which are references to the realm of pure, "extraworldly" consciousness—would indicate, probably, a religious nature.

Beth is young. In a younger group she would have higher scores. Significant in Beth's profile is her relatively high Cm score. But her belief in her ability to make commitments—that is, her capacity to relate herself successfully to the world outside—is not borne out by her perception of time, growth, or love. But if she sees the connections among these four themes, she may be able to use her apparent ability to make commitments for the sake of the other world-relating values. The thought that she is "ready to risk love" may be the right stimulus for growth in Beth. Her low time score, however, might indicate an improper perception of the continuity of consciousness. Time is a central category in existential thought. In fact, it is synonymous with the outward motion of the field of consciousness itself. Her low time score is confirmed, as it were, by her merely average FT score and her generally low ontology score. But because commitment is Beth's highest self-rating, any therapist or philosopher beginning to counsel with her on the basis of the self-assessment of the profile will do well to emphasize her self-perception of being able to make *individual* (I score) *commitments* (Cm score).

Significant in Marilyn's profile—in contrast to Beth's—is her very high time score, a sign that she is experiencing the world as a unified forward-moving continuity, realistically rooted in the here and now. Her time score is supported also by her high FT, TS, and G scores. That support makes her T-score reliable. In any event, it is not common to exaggerate T. We also notice her very low SR, I, E, F, and Lv scores. We have already come across the thought that she is probably basically a very healthy person and can use that health to build up her authenticity. Inauthenticity in her case is learned and probably not very deep-seated. Her high SD item indicates an eager readiness to work with herself. One suspects that Marilyn is a strong and healthy person but still undeveloped. Her inauthenticity is superficial, but the roots of her authenticity seem to be deep indeed. She probably does not understand the full impact of her response to the ontological and methodological questions. But her self-evaluation does indicate, in existential terms, a thoroughly healthy and authentic manner of being-in-the-world. She *is* a field of consciousness, even though she may not understand the full implications of that concept.

Mahlon is also ready to work with himself, as indicated by a high SD score. That goal may be fatuous, however, because he seems spoiled and self-indulgent: he is not willing to accept responsibility for his life (Rs), cannot take pain (P), and seems to have said "no" to life (Li). His inability to reflect (Rf) contradicts his openness for SD. His Difference score is probably experienced as guilt, because of his low Q II score. It may be possible to turn such an interpretation around and point out to him that his Difference score gives him a place to go in life, gives him meaning and the needed challenge for fulfillment. His extremely low freedom score (F), confirmed by an equally low responsibility score (Rs) is a bad omen. He is still a child; he is neither willing nor able to take charge of his life. As a result, his good adaptability score (A) is probably more a sign of spinelessness than strength of survival. But we must grasp every straw of strength—the probably hackneyed goals of growth and self-disclosure. His strengths are not clearly defined. SD, G, and a little I are not enough to support him in the march to authenticity.

Mahlon's profile is saltatory; it jumps all over the place. The impression one gets is that his life is in turmoil, that nothing is settled, and that he lacks the inner resources to deal with what life has to offer him at this time. The only area of consistency, and it is partial at best, is found in his perception of his free will. And what we see is not good; it is an indication of weakness, of enslavement to fate—a theme underscored even more heavily by his extremely low Rs score: He does not feel in control of his life. Additional work in the areas of SD and G (which at least intellectually exist in him) might begin to change the profile dramatically and disclose his real strengths to him.

Another characteristic of Mahlon's profile is that suffering and free will are relatively low, whereas encounter is relatively high. His suffering score is disturbing, an indication he is stopped in life by its negative aspects. He seems to follow the growth movement's opinion that encounter leads to meaning. However, the existential point of view is that the capacity to integrate suffering into a total life and the ability to stand alone are the genuine prerequisites for successful living. Mahlon lacks these qualities at the present.

The situation with Beth is similar. She is average in "encounter" but weak in the integration of suffering. She can expect no progress in self-transcendence until she strengthens her integration of suffering. One asset is that her free will score is average at least.

Marilyn is strong in the encounter dimension, average in the integration of life's negations, low in inner strength. One way for Marilyn to make progress toward authenticity is to increase the Difference score. She must be invited to adopt the existential goals of authenticity intellectually and conceptually. Because the difference is below average, her ambition for authenticity is modest and her perception of the goals that are possible may be inadequate, especially vis-à-vis her healthy potential. Her conceptual goals (answer to Q I) can be raised by additional formal education in the liberal arts. With it, her Difference score can be raised, and new movement can be brought into her life. A good guess is that the first effect of added belletristic education would be to raise her inwardness scores, which will then immediately be reflected in uniformly high scores in the encounter area.

Let us now examine some of the characteristics of Mark's profile. One notices first, perhaps, what is an unusual combination of a high Rf and A self-evaluation. In existential terms this means that Mark probably and correctly perceives himself as having high survival value: he is flexible and adaptable. He is flexible in locating his center between subjectivity and objectivity and he is adaptable in that he can constitute and reconstitute his values and his life-style in accordance with his own decisions. Mark's survival potential is one of his great strengths. It is possible that he may be a troubled man, as was discussed earlier. His capacity for philosophical survival—which he probably does not understand conceptually but practices in actuality—has not only prevented his collapse over these years but also given him an outwardly successful life (M.D., five children, etc.).

A negative feature of Mark's profile is that the bulk of his low scores are in the encounter and self-transcendence area. That G is high while Cm, Lv, and T are low, is a possible indication of where his clue for added strength lies. He seems willing to grow, and the growth that he needs lies in the encounter, in the meeting—of the world and the Other—aspect of human existence.

A strong inwardness score should make strong encounters possible.

But Mark's low Rv score is in the way. And what holds back his reverence for subjectivity is his resistance to self-disclosure (SD) as well as his (professionally based?) rejection of the idea of a consciousness that is not the same as the body (indicated by a low TS rating). The high E rating, which is amazingly out of character with a low TS score, is a highly significant ray of hope.

The constellation of low scores consists of TS, SD, Rv, Cm, and Lv. These are related categories. They must all be raised for authenticity. Mark has the strength to do it, as indicated by his competence in integrating suffering into his life (the most outstanding single area score) and his rather high score in the inwardness area. Mark evidently perceives himself as having considerable inner strength.

Another surprising contradiction is the high G score and the low SD score. These must be brought together to make the process toward authenticity a realistic one. The SD score is likely to be more accurate than the G score. It is possible to give an intellectual and thus meaningless response to item C 13 (G). Item B (SD) elicits more of an experiential response. The contradiction may indicate self-deception.

Mark should start working with whatever theme or area of strength suits him best. It will not take long to discover where that is. He must increase the difference between his concept of life and his actual life, his ideal and his reality (Q I and Q II). That will give him hope. As with Marilyn, it can probably be accomplished, at least in part, through the academic study of a philosophy of man. He has the willpower and self-discipline necessary to achieve philosophic growth, as his free will area indicates.

Mark's profile is his perception of himself; it is a projection, which exaggerates certain features, of how it feels to be him. He is now in a good position to take a fresh look at himself as he himself has projected himself.

Let us now look at a profile with the graph for Q I added to it.

Question I

Let us look at Scott's profile. We notice immediately that his score for Q I is considerably higher than his score in Q II. That is not necessarily to be expected, because we are dealing with statistical averages and not absolute figures. The discrepancy seems to be healthy, in that it gives him meanings toward which to strive. The slopes of the two curves are also similar, with perhaps one interesting exception—there is a crossover, or at least a meeting of lines in the free will area. He is saying to himself that his acceptance (F, Q I) and use (Li, Q I) of freedom, in connection with what he actually lives (F, Q II and Li, Q II) leaves less room for hope, growth, and progress than is the case in any other area of his life. He is stuck in life, his high hopes to the contrary notwithstanding, because he possesses a limited conception of his freedom. That may be the most significant aspect of this profile, a fact borne out by my personal knowledge of the individual. Scott is a bright student, well-informed in existential matters. Nevertheless, he feels paralyzed; he cannot realize what he thinks are his meanings. His profile gives us a clue: ignorance of freedom. Counseling bore out the contention that he did not really understand the enormous possibilities of his human freedom.

Our next focus will be the areas of greatest difference between Q I and Q II scores. These are to be found in the FT, Rs, Cd, SR, I, T, and A scales. The biggest gap is on the I scale. The following descriptive speculations are worth considering. It is his perception (which is far above the average, because on the average the answers to Questions I and II would coincide on the profile) that his sense of being an individual is far less than what it should be. In truth, Scott was a very timid, self-effacing, insecure, and ineffective person. This diagnosis is corroborated by his other high differential scores.

The FT separation shows that whereas conceptually he feels the obligation to experience ego and world as unitary, he does not feel that this is in any way the case. We here have an alienated individual, who believes himself to be cut off from the world. The Rs separation would appear to indicate a puerile, immature avoidance of responsibility for his own life. It suggests a dependent and passive personality. The A gap implies a similar spoiled and self-indulgent childish personality structure. These points of immaturity are further supported by the large SR gap.

What suggestions for therapeutic strategy emerge from this profile? His actual strength (as perceived by him) is P, with possibly the addition of SD, Li, and Rf. A high P would indicate a tragic sense of life, which could either mean inauthentic self-pity or authentic capacity for tolerating and integrating the negativities of life. The latter would be a most commendable strength, one on which a therapist can build. A high score on both SD and Rf would indicate a capacity for therapeutic growth. He probably would be a competent and cooperative patient. A high Li score would indicate that he is motivated to grow in therapy.

These strengths are, in general, corroborated by his scores on Q I. Further, the high Rs and E scores on Q I are worth noting. They indicate the conviction, at least, that the job of growing to authenticity through self-disclosure is fully his responsibility. They also suggest that he is prepared to understand the strength and security that can be derived from an understanding of the nature of our human consciousness, as indicated in items C 6 and C 6a on the Master Table.

If my suggestions for interpretation in this chapter have proven to be inadequate, I suggest that when you are ready to examine your own profile you use your creative imagination and allow your intuition to roam freely. Your personal profile can be highly suggestive in understanding yourself in terms of the categories and themes of existential philosophy.

In the next chapter I will try to illustrate the applications of these analyses into the nature of consciousness to a specific human problem. We will turn to Diana, one of my students, who in her own way epitomizes our universal homelessness. Her philosophical diagnosis, in a word, is homelessness, or alienation of her consciousness from everything, including herself. Our prescription and treatment for her is self-understanding or self-disclosure. These are questions more of philosophy than psychology.

AUTHENTICITY PROFILE

Names: ___

Summary: 1197 1211 399

T-Score	Summary QI	Summary QII	Summary Diff		FT TS Rs / A1 A2 A3 (Ontology)	SD / B (Methodology)	P D Cd / C1 C2 C14 (Suffering)	SR I E Rv / C4 C5 C6 C6a (Inwardness)	F Li / C7 C8 (Free will)	CM Lv T G / C9 C10 C12 C13 (Encounter and self-transcendence)	Rf A / C3 C11 (Survival)
Far Above Average (70)	1152	1064	297	QI	(69) (76) (71)		(68) (70) (66)	(70) (73) (75) (77)		(71) (72) (72)	
				QII	(61) (68) (64)	(69)	(63) (63) (61)	(63) (65) (65) (69)	(68) (65)	(66) (67) (69) (70)	(64) (70)
Above Average (60)	1107	917	194	QI	56 60 58	(61)	57 55 53	55 60 54 60	(61) (61)	57 60 59 (63)	(64) (61)
				QII	50 54 54	57	51 49 48	50 53 47 54	55 53	53 55 56 59	54 58
Average (50)	862	770	92	QI	43 45 44	51	45 41 40	40 47 34 44	47 48	44 49 47 53	49 51
				QII	39 40 43	45	39 36 35	37 42 29 38	43 42	39 42 43 49	45 46
Below Average (40)	717	623	-10	QI	30 30 30	40	34 26 27	35 34 14 28	34 35	31 37 35 43	34 40
				QII	28 25 32	39	27 22 22	24 30 10 22	30 30	26 29 30 38	32 34
Far Below Average (30)	572	476	-118	QI	17 15 17	30	22 11 14	21 21 (-7) 11	21 22	18 26 13 33	20 29
				QII	16 11 21	22	16 8 9	2 19 (-8) 6	17 18	13 16 17 28	21 23
(20)	427	329	-215	QI	4 10 3	19	11 (-6) 1	6 8 (-5)	8 10	5 14 1 23	5 19
	QI	QII	Diff (I–II)	QII	5 7 10	11	4 (-6)(-4)	(-11) 7 (-10)	4 7	(-1) 3 4 17	1 11

WORLD VIEW | PHILOSOPHICAL ANTHROPOLOGY

QI ___
QII ___

Sex: ___ Children: ___
Age: ___
Marital Status: ___
Occupation: ___

AUTHENTICITY PROFILE

Names: ___

Summary: 1197 1211 399

T-Score	Summary QI	Summary QII	Summary Diff		FT TS Rs / A1 A2 A3 (Ontology)	SD / B (Methodology)	P D Cd / C1 C2 C14 (Suffering)	SR I E Rv / C4 C5 C6 C6a (Inwardness)	F Li / C7 C8 (Free will)	CM Lv T G / C9 C10 C12 C13 (Encounter and self-transcendence)	Rf A / C3 C11 (Survival)
Far Above Average (70)	1152	1064	297	QI	(69) (76) (71)		(68) (70) (66)	(70) (73) (75) (77)		(71) (72) (72)	
				QII	(61) (68) (64)	(69)	(63) (63) (61)	(63) (65) (65) (69)	(68) (65)	(66) (67) (69) (70)	(64) (70)
Above Average (60)	1107	917	194	QI	56 60 58	(61)	57 55 53	55 60 54 60	(61) (61)	57 60 59 (63)	(64) (61)
				QII	50 54 54	57	51 49 48	50 53 47 54	55 53	53 55 56 59	54 58
Average (50)	862	770	92	QI	43 45 44	51	45 41 40	40 47 34 44	47 48	44 49 47 53	49 51
				QII	39 40 43	45	39 36 35	37 42 29 38	43 42	39 42 43 49	45 46
Below Average (40)	717	623	-10	QI	30 30 30	40	34 26 27	35 34 14 28	34 35	31 37 35 43	34 40
				QII	28 25 32	39	27 22 22	24 30 10 22	30 30	26 29 30 38	32 34
Far Below Average (30)	572	476	-118	QI	17 15 17	30	22 11 14	21 21 (-7) 11	21 22	18 26 13 33	20 29
				QII	16 11 21	22	16 8 9	2 19 (-8) 6	17 18	13 16 17 28	21 23
(20)	427	329	-215	QI	4 10 3	19	11 (-6) 1	6 8 (-5)	8 10	5 14 1 23	5 19
	QI	QII	Diff (I–II)	QII	5 7 10	11	4 (-6)(-4)	(-11) 7 (-10)	4 7	(-1) 3 4 17	1 11

WORLD VIEW | PHILOSOPHICAL ANTHROPOLOGY

QI ___
QII ___

Sex: ___ Children: ___
Age: ___
Marital Status: ___
Occupation: ___

5:

Diana

Diana's Letter

Below is a moving letter from Diana; eventually she requested that I discuss her problems in class. Diana could be very attractive, but is at present very much overweight. She seems to know, instinctively, that philosophy will assist her in understanding her many problems and helpfully support her in resolving her tragic agony. Understandably her problems are deeply disturbing to her and in this letter she has not much hope.

Diana suffers from a severe case of alienation. Let us hear from her directly. Following is her letter, unedited.

Dear Dr. Koestenbaum:

First of all I must say that I am afraid that you might make fun of what I have to say. If the following is inane or irrelevant to this course, please pass it by. I am afraid of you. Your existence, like a blinding light diminishes my existence into darkness because I am not quite real yet.

Now to get to the subject of my concern. I would like to discuss guilt. You say that guilt is good because it means that you have made a decision but what if that guilt paralyzes your life? Perhaps the presence of guilt means that you have not accepted the responsibility for your decision.

I have two major guilts that have in fact paralyzed my life and closed me up inside myself afraid to take from life (people) or give to life (people). One of these guilts is connected with my child who was born out of wed lock. She is now four years old and I now regret that I did not give her up for adoption by a woman and a man who could give her the things I can not. I feel inadequate as a mother but am unwilling to give her up now because she is part of me—I am part of her—she is a reminder of my sexuality, my fertility and selfishly I am unwilling to give that reminder up. This is my decision but my guilt burrows into my heart like a tick and I cannot breathe.

My second guilt is my feeling of responsibility for my fathers death. He walked in on my boyfriend and I when we were in bed making love. He blew up, raged then escaped to the obscurity of alcohol for three days, after which he returned home and consumed a bottle of sleeping pills. I have for these past two years felt responsible for his suicide. This has paralyzed my personal life. I have been unable to have a meaningful relationship with another human being since then. I want to give but feel incapable of it.

These two guilts have led me to depths of despair out of which I have not yet been able to rise out of. My life is meaningless. My existence is less than a single tear drop in the vastness of humanities existence. No one needs me in this world. I am essential to no one. I am cold, afraid and alone. But what frightens me more than my own loneliness is the realization that we are *all* lonly sad creatures pathetically reaching out for contact. Perhaps it is the search that provides meaning for existence and not the attainment of the goal. If this is so then we must all keep reaching.

For your time, I thank you, Dr. Koestenbaum.

Diana

In this touching letter are reflected thousands of suffering human beings. In a manner of speaking, we all see part of ourselves in Diana. We must therefore reach out to her, as we also reach out to ourselves, with the warmth of our compassion and the strength of our determination.

Before I can help Diana with her problems, I must help her understand the letter she wrote. Thus, before she analyzes the *content* of her letter she must be helped to examine its *form*. As a matter of fact, the problems disturb her so much that she alternately quivers, and is paralyzed as she attempts to discuss her problems privately with me. Her whole being is deeply *involved* with her guilts, her inadequacies, and her despair, with her late father, her daughter, and her own overweight body. She is so *close* to her suffering that she *is* her suffering.

As the first step, then, she must be encouraged and even urged to step out of the deep involvement with her body and her problems and look at her whole life situation with ascetic detachment. She must disengage her mind from her anxiety so that she can reflect on it and discuss it. I invited her to read her letter to me out loud. Before we move on, a warning is in order.

Cautions

I use the following cautions whenever I ask a student or client to read his statement of self-disclosure out loud. I do the same when I read the statement of a problem to a class, which I do frequently with the materials students submit to me. These cautions are a declaration of respect and reverence for the precious inwardness of my students. These then are the prerequisites for sharing an individual's problems with others:

1. I must have the unqualified permission of the student or client to discuss all aspects of the material presented. If anything is to be held in confidence I must be told and I will always respect it. In fact, one person wrote me a letter in which she said the following:

> I am writing to ask for a private consultation. You have told me you prefer to work in groups and I can understand your preference.
> I have several reasons for wanting privacy. One I think that I have always had a problem trusting people. Since I have taken several classes from you, over a period of perhaps ten years and in all that time you have never revealed a confidence—I believe that you have my trust.

This letter indicated how important trust and confidence can be.

2. I will often distort the facts in a letter to insure added privacy to the writer. Because I use these letters in public lectures or classes or groups, such distortion seems only fair.

3. If anyone else benefits from the discussion of a private problem, I thank the writer. He permits us to learn through an act of courage, risk, and some self-sacrifice. That act is to be appreciated with gratitude.

4. If the writer wishes to come forward and identify himself, speak for himself, and establish a dialogue with me, he can and must make that decision entirely on his own and assume full responsibility for it. My share of the dialogue is to be sensitive, helpful, and kind.

5. I point out that in discussing a "case" we are really discussing a throbbing human life and not a disembodied intellectual abstraction. Because I usually ask for problems that are (1) agonizing and (2) without specific solution, I recognize how deeply sensitive the material is with which we deal. I expect all of us to approach the discussion with the reverence and respect that is demanded by the dignity of another human being.

6. I am guarded about my reactions, analyses, and interpretations.

My comments are intended to elicit discussion and reflection. They are not pompous statements about insights regarding eternal truths that I might have. The test of truth lies in the suffering individual and not in the external observer.

7. Finally, I compliment the writer on the courage and the seriousness with which he approaches his life.

Diana's Discoveries

Let us now return to Diana and her letter. I urged her not only to hear her voice but also to think of the letter as coming from someone else. In existential philosophy I call this first step in self-understanding "reflection" rather than "being." I have here invoked the principle of reflection from the Master Table ("I am able both to *live* my life and to *reflect* on my life"). I point out to her that as she reads her statement and thinks of it as coming from another person she *reflects* on herself and her letter rather than merely *being* herself and her life. She is now no longer the Diana in the letter but also the *detached observer* of the Diana in the letter.

This deceptively simple act of reflection has nevertheless the potential for marvelous strength-giving and even therapeutic powers. You can do the same by talking *about* your problem rather than by *having* or *living* your problem.

Even before she goes into any details of her problem—that is, before she analyzes the content of her letter—she has, by listening to herself, made several important discoveries with wide application.

HOPE

Reflection leads her now to her first big insight: There is always hope. By *reflecting* on her life instead of *being* her life she has discovered hope. She sees her life in perspective; she can fit it into the larger world of which she is a part. Inevitably, the problem is thereby diminished. She now says, "I can think of worse things!" "I am thankful I have a lovely daughter!" "How beautiful it is that I am still living and not dead like my father!" The beauties of nature now become sacred gifts to her. Perspective always gives hope. She discovers that there are no truly hopeless situations. She learns that the secret of finding the hopeful ingredient in any situation, no matter how desperate, is to see it in perspective. And Diana's secret of perspectival vision is to force herself to be detached—however briefly—from her problems: to look at them rather than to be involved in them.

By merely reflecting on her behavior, she has made a discovery that is generic to man and of the deepest concern to all men of all nations in all the ages of history: the need for and the reality of hope.

Hope is the knowledge that I am time, that the consciousness and the ego that I *am* is in truth the forward movement in time. Hope means that the future is real and is mine. Hopelessness, on the other hand, is the illusion that I am *not* time, that time does not exist. Diana has discovered the truth of the principles of time and of growth ("I experience time as living in a present which, while utilizing the past, connects directly and primarily into my future," and "My life is an endless process of growing, emerging, and reaching out"). The more she integrates that truth into her daily life, the healthier she will be.

Later I will suggest some exercises that help achieve a sense of time, future and, growth.

ACTION

Reflection now leads Diana to a second major discovery: she has already *acted* to help herself. She has not only written about her suffering, she has done much more. The action of writing down her problem in itself gave her some perspective and distance. But beyond that, *she acted in submitting the problem to me and having it discussed,* even though anonymously, first privately and then with the class. Reflecting on her letter, she discovers it as more than a letter: it is an *action* that has enabled her to put herself in touch with the very world from which she had been alienated! Diana's writing is already part of Diana's solution. She has now discovered that she can make a commitment and thereby has already overcome in part her deep alienation. She has discovered the principle of *commitment* from the Master Table. She has established identification and contact with the world of people that heretofore seemed inaccessible to her. In a manner of speaking, she has already achieved the goal she seeks: communication, contact, being extroverted in the world rather than introverted in an alienated self.

The discovery that she can act—indeed, that the act is a *fait accompli*—is also the discovery that her isolating alienation from the world has already begun to be overcome. To have acted, rather than merely to have thought, is to have overcome the gap between self and world that characterizes mental illness. To have acted is to have built a firm bridge between the formerly isolated, depressed, and ineffectual self and the real and permanent world beyond. When Diana recognizes that she, an insular ego, has made a commitment to the world around her by the simple expedient of submitting her letter and reading it out loud, she is able to understand the essential nature of human existence, as expressed in the field theory of man ("I am neither a body nor a soul but a continuous consciousness-body-world field").

A small rock jutting above the waves of the ocean has now been recognized by her to be but the peak of an enormous underwater mountain. The small rock is her small act of submitting a letter for discussion. The vast mountain that it reveals is the truth about man, the field-of-consciousness theory of man. Diana now discovers that the vast underwater mountain has other peaks that show above the surface many miles away from the first. To Diana this insight means she can act in other areas of her life as well. She can act not only by submitting a letter but also by raising her daughter, establishing new and healthy relations with men, and making meaningful contact with the academic environment in which she is living at present.

THE CENTER

Furthermore, the principle of reflection leads Diana to a third discovery, one that is as important as it is difficult to understand. In reflecting on her problem—as opposed to being steeped in it—Diana has discovered her true philosophic center; she has uncovered the roots of her genuine support and her true foundation. She has discovered her pure consciousness, her untarnished awareness. She is now in the presence of an insight as ancient and as venerable as mankind itself. She recognizes that her true nature, her true self, is not her paralysis, her guilt about her father, her inadequacy as a mother, or even her overweight body. On the contrary, her true self and nature—the authentic Diana—is *the distance from* her insufferable world; and this distance is *created by the act of reflection itself.* The magic power of reflection is ancient wisdom in the history of mankind (Eastern mystics and Western ascetics) and it is also a recent discovery in psychotherapy (the power of talking *about* our problems). Great revolutions are based on simple ideas.

A swimmer in the water is at one with the water. A swimmer outside the water, looking at it from a distance, knows that in truth he is different from the water. Diana has discovered for herself the truth and the importance of the principle of eternity from the Master Table ("There exists a consciousness within me which I am and which is eternal").

Civilization has called that psychological distance manifested by the magic act of reflection on one's troubles the *self* or *consciousness, spirit* or *awareness,* even *ego, subjectivity,* and *inwardness,* and sometimes the *soul.* The fact remains that the principle of reflection shows to us our genuine center, the awareness or consciousness that we in reality are. All health, all joy and happiness begins in that spiritual center. All of Diana's strength, power, and independence, all control over her life and over her destiny, all these have their roots in her spiritual or conscious center. And Diana made the discovery of the nature of her consciousness by the simple act of reading her letter as if it were someone else's. She learned to *look at* herself rather than to *be* herself.

What this means is that she is now already in touch with the source of all her strength and with the foundation of her security. She has tapped her inner reservoir of power, which can give her meaning by overcoming her alienation. A metaphor will help.

You see a movie that touches you deeply, and the tears stream down your cheeks. You and the movie are one. What happens on the screen happens to you. But that is your false self: in reality you are of course not on the screen. Suddenly you realize that your weeping is seen by someone whose observation of your emotion embarrasses you. Instantly your oneness with the movie situation disappears and your center, your true self, is experienced to be at a distance from the screen. You console yourself by saying, "It is just a movie; I am different from the movie." It is that distance which discloses to you the pure consciousness that is you. That is the meaning of reflection.

The same access to your inward center is made possible if the movie scares you. While you are in the state of being terrified, you are one with the movie. You can forcibly disengage yourself from this total identification by realizing that you are only observing a movie and are not immersed in it. Once you succeed, you have achieved the sense of control and peace that comes with the distance of reflection. As you are scared by the movie, you say to yourself "It's only a movie; it is not reality." In this way, you move from illusion (identity with the movie) to reality (distance from the movie). And now remember that you are the distance between the screen and your ego; that distance is your true self.

Diana has come home.

POWER

Finally, *Diana has discovered the nature of her true self*—that is, the pure consciousness that is man. She has understood experientially the truth of the fact that her inner self is her home and her dignity, which is the principle of reverence ("Each individual human inward subjectivity is the divine consciousness in man"). She has also understood that she is in reality two selves ("I am a pure consciousness that has a psychological personality, a physical body, and many social roles"). She is Diana the observer of her problems and Diana the problem itself. To clarify this point is somewhat more difficult than to explain Diana's other discoveries.

The completed act of reflection discloses to Diana the fundamental philosophical fact that a human being is an independent consciousness *in addition* to being a person, a body, and a series of social roles.

While Diana is *reflecting* on her performance—as she does when we discuss it—she is not the Diana who *has* the problems, nor is she the Diana who "looks at," "knows," "understands," "sees," and "perceives" the Diana with the problems. There are two Dianas in existence here. One is the empirical Diana, the Diana with problems, anxieties, and depression. The other is the transcendental Diana—Diana the observer. Diana the observer is pure consciousness, pure self, pure ego. That Diana *is not* a problem, *does not have* a problem, but is a neutral observer *looking at* the Diana with problems. Diana has now understood the second aspect of the philosophical nature of man—the distinction between the transcendental and the empirical egos.

She is now in a position to acquire the sense of security and rootedness that comes from recognizing her true self as inward consciousness, and this is the principle of self-reliance ("I am an adult consciousness that exists alone: I choose to be independent and self-reliant"). In that consciousness lie all her strengths and her answers.

As an exercise, the reader should examine a real and serious problem of his own and test whether or not for him making the above discoveries and having the corresponding experiences has the same therapeutic effect that it had on Diana.

Diana has accomplished significant existential achievements. Through the extremely simple device of reflection, she has made significant and helpful discoveries, all of which have their foundation in reputable existential philosophy. The principle of reflection states, "I am able both to *live* my life and to *reflect* on my life." She reflected on her problem by writing it down, by reading her letter out loud and pretending it was written by another and by sharing the letter with someone she trusted, and, finally, by hearing it read in class. As a consequence, Diana has already achieved several insightful and therapeutic experiences. She has discovered that there is real hope for her; that she can act—that is, that she already has in fact overcome her alienation from the world; and she has discovered her true conscious self—the free spirit or consciousness that she is—and that this consciousness is her home, where she has her roots. These discoveries have universal validity; they are the philosophical truths about human beings in general. In short:

1. I am respected.
2. I have hope.
3. I can act to improve my life.
4. I am in touch with the world (I have overcome alienation).
5. I am in touch with my center.
6. I am strong.
7. I have found my home.

Let us now examine—*for content,* not form—a paragraph of Diana's letter, and learn from this analysis, for her sake and ours, how to turn despair into hope and failure into success.

Strengths

In order for us to help Diana we must point out her strengths. She has many, and they are real. She ends her letter with a profound insight:

> But what frightens me more than my own loneliness is the realization that we are *all* lonly sad creatures pathetically reaching out for contact. Perhaps it is the search that provides meaning for existence and not the attainment of the goal. If this is so then we must all keep reaching.

She is here informing us not what frightens her most but rather of the source of her hope. This is one unmistakable evidence of her strength.

She announces, first of all, that she will solve the problem herself. "Perhaps it is the search that provides meaning for existence and not the attainment of the goal. If this is so then we must all keep reaching." She does not expect others to solve her problems for her because she already possesses the strength to say "yes" to life and to reconstruct it into happier habits. That strength is a sign of great health. She may have a more difficult life than that experienced by other young women; however, she fully measures up to the occasion by *telling us* that she will solve her own problems. What a privilege for us to be permitted to witness such a beautiful expression of strength, life-affirmation, and courage under these painful circumstances!

Diana, in the second place, has used the principle of life ("My first and last choice is to say 'yes' to life"). To say "yes" to life is not an automatic act: It is a *choice* that all of us can make. And Diana has made that choice. Had she ended her letter in despair or with threats of suicide, her choice would have been to say "no" to life. She says "yes" in her determination to succeed, in her will to be happy, and in her choosing hope over despair.

We all possess that power. It is the power of freedom and it is expressed in theme C 7 ("I always choose because I am always free"). Some of us use our freedom to choose despair and to give up, whereas others choose to fight, win, and conquer.

Third, Diana demonstrates deep philosophical wisdom—that is, insight into an eternal truth—when she writes, "We are *all* lonly sad creatures pathetically reaching out for contact. . . . We must all keep reaching." She has discovered the universal human truth of the principle of self-reliance ("I am an adult consciousness that exists alone: I choose to be independent and self-reliant"). She has thereby discovered that human beings are a brotherhood of aliens and a commune of strangers. She has uncovered the ancient wisdom that although man is totally alone in this world he nevertheless can lovingly share that tragedy with others.

As a result, she knows, fourth, the meaning of love, kindness, compassion, and intimacy as expressed in principle C 10 ("As an adult I can choose to meet, confront, witness, understand, and be mirrored by another; I can also choose to love and care for that person"), even though she has not yet been able to integrate it meaningfully into her actual life. Diana may be totally alone, but she also knows that everyone else is likewise totally alone. And thus she understands that in the pathos of suffering, human beings get close, meet each other, love and respect each other, and achieve a sense of genuine intimacy. (I will deal more fully with the concepts of pain and tragedy in future chapters.) The beauty of being accepted and of accepting another human being unconditionally—that is, the beauty of both loving and being loved—is possible only on a foundation of aloneness and a sharing of suffering.

Fifth, Diana has a feeling for the tragic sense of life, which leads her to insights into the principles of pain and death ("I choose to value my pains" and "I choose to value my limitations"). Only by understanding how painfully alone she is and how all others are equally painfully alone can she understand the meaning of the existential way of life. We thus can point out to Diana her real strengths, strengths whose existence is an inspiration to all those who have the good sense to perceive them. Her basic health rests on the fact that her letter of alienation nevertheless discloses real understanding of the principles of the Master Table, and with it of the existential way of life.

We learn from Diana's strengths the following:

1. When in despair, recognize and list your strengths.
2. You have the power to say "yes" to life. Use it!
3. If you feel alone, remember that we all are alone.
4. You can overcome loneliness by *sharing* loneliness. If you are able to reflect on yourself—get out of yourself—then you are also worthy and capable of love.
5. If you understand the tragic sense of life you have the potential for maturity and authenticity.

6:

Diana's Guilt

The Meaning of Guilt

Let us now discuss Diana's guilt. We all suffer guilt and a compassionate philosophy must address itself to that problem. The existential principles of the Master Table can be used to remove neurotic obstacles and help fulfill your human potential.

Not all guilt experiences are the same: some are bad, unhealthy, and destructive. They paralyze action, stunt growth, and may even lead to the deep depressions that end in suicide. Other guilt experiences are constructive and healthy. "Bad guilt," which the existential personality theory calls neurotic or pathological guilt, can be cured. "Good guilt," which is called existential or ontological guilt, cannot be cured. This latter guilt is in the essence of man. Ontological guilt experiences are natural and inevitable. To remove or "cure" existential guilt is like curing high blood pressure by draining the blood, or curing shortness of breath by surgically removing the lungs.

Guilt is, for Diana, a pervasive state of mind. To deal with her guilt and the life-style produced by it, she must first confront and meet directly her experiences and feelings of guilt. She must get into her guilt, feel it fully and in detail rather than escape it. She must not fear her guilt feelings but have the courage to open herself up to them. That activity itself involves an understanding of the rule for self-disclosure ("I must be fully disclosed to myself both as a human being and as *Diana*") as well as of the principles of death and limits from the Master Table. The guilty person can gain strength, maturity, and joy as the result of a direct confrontation with that kind of guilt.

"Bad" guilt is "neurotic"; "good" guilt is "existential." And Diana has both kinds of guilt. In helping Diana, we must show her that her guilts about her illicit affair, her father's death, her illegitimate daughter, her incompetence as a mother, and her failure as a friend and lover all contain in them a grain of wisdom, a portion of universal truth about the human condition. She is in error if she thinks of her guilt as "all bad." Her guilt can reveal to Diana the universal truth of the human condition. It can lead to insight. Guilt is a means to self-disclosure, and the wisdom thus gained can make one free.

In general, suffering and pain can be for Diana—as they have been for many human beings—the foundation of what is deep and meaningful in life. Suffering and pain can push open the doors to health-giving philosophical knowledge about man and his world. Rather than think of Diana's guilt merely as an illness, we must also recognize that it is rich in creative and constructive truths about man's eternal essence. It other words, there is a cosmic dimension to Diana's suffering. She is sitting on a treasure, and does not know it.

Let us point up that portion of Diana's guilt that is healthy (existential) and examine the notion of existential guilt as it applies to Diana.

Freedom and Polarity

If Diana feels guilty, it is not only because she violated a rule: she feels guilty because she *is* guilty, and she *is* guilty because she has exercised her freedom. She recognizes this in her letter, but only conceptually, not experientially. Guilt is a pain to be valued and not a feeling to be repressed or tranquilized. *Guilt is proof that one has used and is now using one's freedom.* In short, guilt is proof of one's authenticity. Only computers feel no guilt. He who has no sense of guilt should worry. He has no surface evidence of being free—no evidence of decision-making, no evidence of the intuition that he could have chosen differently and independently, no evidence of responsibility for his self-determined actions.

What distinguishes Diana—and all of us—from animals? The fact that she is free; the fact that she makes choices and decisions, that she can create an identity for herself and for her child, that she can choose to do and she can also choose not to do. Her freedom makes Diana human. In fact, it is her freedom that makes Diana, and the rest of us, godlike. To choose means to say "yes" to one thing by saying "no" to another. Diana chose a sexual affair rather than a nonsexual life. In saying "yes" to sex she said "no" to celibacy. The sense of joy resulted from yes-saying, whereas the sense of guilt derives from no-saying: To the extent that Diana said "yes" to sex with her boyfriend, she experienced joy, but to the extent she said *no* to the rules of premarital celibacy she felt guilt. Joy is proof of a decision made, but so is guilt. Her guilt is but the realization that she made a decision. And decision-making is an authentic, free, and human activity.

The practical consequence of knowing about existential guilt is a new mindset. Before philosophy Diana insistently demanded, unconsciously, that she get rid of her guilt. She felt *defective* because of her guilt (she felt guilty about her guilt). Now, after philosophy, she feels *adequate* because of her guilt. She has learned to live with it. She has learned to feel comfortable and real *because* she feels guilt, resting peacefully, as it were, supported by the couch that is her guilt.

If Diana's actions had been reversed and she had abstained from sex with her boyfriend, the basic joy-guilt pattern would have remained unchanged. Then her joy would have been based on consistency with her father's principles and the rules of society; her joy would have then been in the affirmation of "character" and "obedience." Because she violated these rules by sleeping with her boyfriend, she is guilty. The options were society and father against boyfriend and sex. She chose the latter. Knowing she could have used her freedom to choose the former makes her feel guilty.

Nothing would be changed if she had chosen otherwise. Let us assume she used her freedom to choose society and father rather than boyfriend and sex. Her guilt would now be that of unfulfilled possibilities; this would have been a free decision against expressing her feminine sexuality. Again she would have made a choice: duty over love. Again she would experience an ambiguous mixture of joy and guilt. Seeing that guilt is inevitable transforms Diana's perception of the meaning of guilt from something sick and destructive to something human, healthy, and elevating. In her very guilt can be the seeds of her happiness.

We learn from these analyses that the joy-guilt, yes-no oscillation is the essence of life itself. It is not true that Diana would be without guilt if she had lived differently. To be alive, to be conscious, and to be a self or an ego, to exist in this world, is to be in a state of stress. Polarization is natural. Diana has recognized the truth of the principle of contradiction: "The inescapable ambiguities and contradictions of life are my powerful allies." As we saw in Chapter 2, life is like a magnet—without the stress between the positive and the negative poles there can exist no magnetic field in the first place. Consciousness itself is in its essence like a magnetic field. These are messages of hope rather than despair, of health and maturity rather than of sickness and inadequacy. Philosophy has helped Diana turn weakness into strength and despair into hope.

Conclusions

How can you learn from Diana's guilt? When you feel oppressed with guilt, remember the following:

1. Guilt is proof of freedom.
2. All life is conflict.

3. Your agony is normal rather than sick, existential rather than neurotic.
4. The existence of your guilt proves that you have
    a. the strength to *make decisions,*
    b. the strength to *evaluate* your own life by your own standards,
    c. the strength to *choose* and *maintain* your own standards and values.

We will examine each one of Diana's guilts separately to see what they teach us. She has four: (1) guilt about sex with her boyfriend, (2) guilt about her father's death, (3) guilt about her inadequacy as a mother, and (4) guilt about her inadequacy as a human being.

We have already discussed the first of these and derived the insight that her philosophical experiences will be essentially unchanged whichever way she chooses. She thus gains the courage to make her own decisions and establish her own evaluations. Let us now consider her guilt about her father.

Her Father's Death

The matter of her father's death, appearances to the contrary notwithstanding, is not a complicated matter. From an objective point of view it is of course completely clear that she is not responsible for her father's death. Instead, she has *chosen* to hold herself responsible; she *wants* to be responsible for his death. One traditional —that is, nonexistential—psychological approach to Diana's guilt might run as follows: "You are not responsible for your father's death. You can get rid of these feelings of responsibility—that is, your guilt feelings—by seeing the situation objectively. Psychotherapy can help you rid yourself of that guilt. The guilt is the introjection of external rules." An existential approach tells Diana: "Your guilt feelings are valid. You can be helped to perceive them as healthy and strong rather than as sick and weak."

In this context, she must remember the principles of both freedom and responsibility. In other words, Diana must assume *subjective* responsibility for the death of her father, but this is a responsibility over which she exercises full control, which she adopts freely and rationally. It is not a responsibility which controls her as if she were a marionette, because it is not externally imposed. Although she is not responsible objectively, she must make his death hers, subjectively. In truth, she already *has* made his death hers—she already *has* assumed responsibility for it, hence her painful feelings.

The situation is similar to the responsibility for a dream. Objectively speaking, I am not responsible for the content of my dreams. If I seek authenticity, however, I must choose to assume responsibility for all aspects of my dreams. Then I am ready to learn from them and use them therapeutically.

Thus, Diana is not responsible for her father's death in any objective, moral, and legal sense. Nevertheless, she must take full existential responsibility for his death if she wishes to gain control over her life. This decision is tricky business; but it is a crucial one. We must spend time reflecting on it.

Underlying Diana's guilt feelings about her father's death are the natural human resentments, violent feelings, and even hate and wishes for the death of one's parents. These are not sick, but normal feelings, and understanding them can be constructive in plumbing one's own depths with the help of existential philosophy. Diana's disturbing death-wishes toward her father represented a choice. But her decision, far deeper than ordinary memory or psychotherapy can take her, to hate her father and wish him dead, is not necessarily an evil one, for it does not kill. In fact, a person who has a clear perception of this fantasy wish and recognizes it as normal can as a result have an excellent real relationship with his parent. It is the person who hides this wish deeply in his consciousness who is likely to have neurotic interchanges with his parents. Diana feels guilty because she did not love her father as she feels she should have; on the contrary, she hated him and wished him symbolically dead. And, true enough, her father answered her wish by actually dying. Her guilt is thus about an act or choice—the wish to have him dead. But even that wish is independent of any action her father might have taken.

The *philosophical* meaning of Diana's guilt is this: She chose her father's death. She is as responsible as if she had actually killed him. That, however, is the language of her inward consciousness, not that of the moral or the legal system.

INDEPENDENCE

But why is Diana's responsibility for the death-wish of her father existentially important? *That Diana chooses to wish her father dead means that she affirms her own independence and difference.* By wishing him dead she is asserting her uniqueness; she announces that she is different from her father, that she is an individual. She says "yes" to herself through the device of saying "no" to the world. The underground shoots from the old tree have given rise elsewhere to a new tree. The connecting shoots can now rot or be cut; they are no longer needed. In fact, they interfere with the independent development of each separate tree. Diana has now discovered that *her guilt about her dead father is really the choice of her own independence.* She has discovered the meaning of the principles of self-reliance and individuality and she has used them ("I am an adult consciousness that exists alone: I choose to be independent and self-reliant," and "It is right and normal for me to seem different from other human beings").

Diana misunderstood her guilt feelings. She misunderstood the meaning of the secret death-wish of her father: It was not a psychotic wish for *his* death but a healthy demand for *her* independence. The unfortunate circumstance of his actual death confused her decision. Philosophy can help her sort out her thoughts. Before philosophy she felt sick and paralyzed over her decision to kill the father within her. After philosophy she feels healthy and mobile over that decision.

The symbols of independence—which for her include the sin of symbolic patricide—do not kill; on the contrary, they can help create a superbly mature relationship between the living daughter and her real father. It is the repression of the symbols for independence that can kill by eliminating the distance between subject and object. That distance in each of us guarantees rational knowledge and emotional control. The elimination of that distance creates a dangerous psychopathology.

It must be made clear to Diana that in analyzing the guilt about her father's death she has in fact made a fundamental philosophical discovery about human nature. The death-wish toward a parent and its ensuing guilt are not proof of illness but the expression that there exists at the center of consciousness an authentic choice of self-affirmation, independence, and self-reliance. The philosophic insight into the revealing nature of that guilt leads Diana from an immature and neurotic perception of the daughter-father relationship to a mature and authentic person-to-person perception.

Gradually, Diana is recognizing the innate health, maturity, normalcy, and strength that naturally reside in her soul. As a result, she is now less likely than before to deprecate herself. Moreover, she has gained immense self-confidence merely by recognizing herself in a true philosophic light. No external facts have changed in Diana's life by virtue of this existential analysis of her consciousness. What has changed dramatically is her perception of her life. Its interpretation and meaning have been transformed. What before was sickness is now seen to contain a significant core of health. In fact, what appears to be sickness may in actual fact be an essential ingredient in health. What earlier was weakness is now seen to hide strength. And what once was ugliness and worthlessness is now recognized to contain beauty and dignity. Philosophic self-knowledge has accomplished that conversion for Diana.

Harry's Patricide

How can one manage guilt? Socrates said "Know thyself." The goal of the philosophical life is self-disclosure—that is, an understanding that is as complete as possible of oneself and of how he is situated in the world. Diana must therefore understand what is behind her guilt about her father's death.

The question of how to accomplish this can be illustrated with the case of Harry. At 39, he is a successful research biochemist in Stockton, California. When he was only seven, he witnessed his father being bludgeoned to death by a robber who had broken into his family's house. As part of the therapy to help him discover deeper layers of meaning and insight behind that experience, Harry was submerged in a warm whirlpool bath, then rocked until he could recall and relive those early terrifying memories. What he recalled went far beyond ordinary memory, all the way to the philosophic foundations of human existence. At first he recalled his fright and despair at the loss. Then Harry began to discover the horrible truth that at one level of his being he had actually wanted and needed his father dead; thus the memory of the murder was worse than he expected because it was a wish or a prediction come true. But why did Harry *want* his father dead? He *had* loved his father! Was Freud right, and was it true that little Harry was jealous of the relationship between his father and his mother? Perhaps the Oedipal situation did exist and perhaps it does account for his death-wish. Harry had been willing to accept that psychoanalytic interpretation, but nevertheless, it did not remove his symptoms. His life was still meaningless. In being led back to even greater spiritual depths, Harry discovered that the secret death-wish for his father was not only a matter of early childhood but remained with him throughout his entire life. What did that mean?

Harry did not want his real father dead—the flesh and blood person, the human being with inalienable rights for life, liberty, and the pursuit of happiness. He wanted that father dead whom he had swallowed into his own being, his personal center. And that father has to die for all of us. Harry needed to affirm his independence, his uniqueness, his *difference* from and lack of dependence on the world. His human essence is to demonstrate that he is not someone else. In direct and simple symbols, that independence becomes the metaphor of Harry killing his own father.

When Harry discovered that his pain about his father's death and his subsequent feelings of inadequacy (rooted in the fact that he was now fatherless and thus considered himself less of a person) were really guilt about needing to kill the father that had entered and appropriated his being, he screamed. He screamed: "Dad, *I* killed you because I wanted to kill you. *I* murdered you, because I wanted to murder you." And he ended the session with profound sobs of relief.

Harry had made the central philosophic discovery that, in order to be the sanctity that is his center, he must expel all foreign matter. By confusing symbol with reality (the symbol was his father and the reality was his independence) he burdened his life with needless pain and stultifying restrictions. In the "philosophic therapy" he reached the philosophic foundation of his being and discovered the insight that many wise men have found: he disclosed his consciousness to himself. The calm center, as with a hurricane, exists only after all foreign matter is hurled outside. Harry had discovered the holiness of his center and with that discovery he became a mature adult.

Conclusions

Let us now return to Diana's guilt about her father's death. She must make a parallel discovery. In the simplest language possible, the following points must become clear to her:

1. In objective terms, she is not responsible for her father's death; he is responsible for his daughter's maladjustments. The rightful expectation is that the parent know how to cope with life and produce healthy children.

2. Diana must not ignore or deny her guilt; it is real and important. Negative experiences disclose the truth about man—through them man can be his guilt; move into it; feel and think through it. Diana can do that herself, in part, by deliberately developing fantasies and daydreams about her guilt.

3. By identifying herself with her guilt, Diana moves from guilt as paralysis (neurotic guilt) to guilt as self-disclosure (existential guilt).

4. Her guilt can translate itself into a choice, a decision, a free act, or a deliberate wish. It can be transformed into her decision to fantasy-kill her father, to become an independent freedom, a free inwardness, an ego, and a center. And that decision is one of supreme authenticity. She needs the guilt about her father's death to experience the power of her freedom. She herself has freely earned her independence. That is the meaning of her guilt about her father.

The general lessons for you are:

1. You are not responsible for the decisions of others.

2. Guilt is real and important.

3. Be your guilt; identify with it; it will give you strength.

4. Assume fully the responsibility that your guilt suggests. It will make you independent.

But Diana also feels guilty because she is an inadequate mother.

Miserable Motherhood

On the basis of the evidence in the letter, Diana *is* inadequate as a mother. She seems to hate her daughter just as much as she obviously hates herself today, hated herself as a child, and perhaps as much as she herself was hated as a child. Her daughter does not exist in her own right as a human being with needs, individuality, and integrity. Diana is not able to see her little girl as an individual any more than her father recognized her right to independence. Why not? Because she does not see herself as an individual. Diana does not think of herself as an inwardness who deserves care, love, and esteem. Apparently, her daughter exists only to satisfy her: "but I am unwilling to give her up now because she is part of me—I am part of her—she is a reminder of my sexuality, my fertility and selfishly am unwilling to give that reminder up." Evidently, people are to be used and not to be encountered.

Diana has chosen to deny her daughter, just as she has chosen to deny herself, because in denying her daughter she denies herself as a mother: "I now regret that I did not give her up for adoption."

The facts are clear. Diana has no concept of herself as a subjectivity, as an inwardness, as a person, or as a solid individual. She thinks of herself as a thing, as an object, therefore she sees others, including her daughter, also as objects. Her daughter exists to give her pleasure, just as Diana has existed all these years to give others pleasure. The time has come for her to understand the meaning of *meeting* another consciousness as opposed to *using* that other consciousness; to understand the truth of the principle of love: "As an adult I can choose to meet, confront, witness, understand, and be mirrored by another. I can also choose to love and care for that person." The movement from seeing people as things to that of recognizing them as inward subjectivities is a transformation as dramatic as the evolution from monkey to man.

Here, in the relationship with her daughter, Diana's guilt means far more than proof of the exercise of freedom: she has used her freedom in the most pernicious way of all—to deny herself and another. Being a mother means being Diana—and she has denied being a mother. She has used her freedom to destroy herself! Diana is three things: a woman, a mother, and an ex-child. In denying her own living child she in fact chooses to reject the woman in her; because woman gives birth to child, she chooses to reject the mother in her; and she denies the beauty of being a child—whether that child is herself or her little girl—because she wanted to give up her daughter.

But Diana is *choosing* these denials—they are not automatic. And choosing them is choosing to say "no" to important aspects of life. She is rejecting the principle of life: "My first and last choice is to say 'yes' to life." However, if she knows she has the power to say "no," she knows she also has the power to say "yes." She must now resolve —and act on that resolve—to ally herself with her womanhood, motherhood, and childhood.

It is, strictly speaking, false to say that Diana is inadequate as a mother, but it is true that she chooses to destroy herself. And that destruction can be the downfall of both Diana and her daughter. Once she perceives her life in this dismal perspective (the destroyer of herself and her daughter) and her previous insights give her the strength and courage to face the bitter truth about herself, she can use the freedom that destroys and change it into a freedom that creates. She must choose herself as a woman-mother-child. She must tell her daughter she loves her and devote her life to making her into a mature and authentic human being.

How does she tell her daughter all these things? By spending time with her, by being rational, tolerant, and affectionate, by being devoted and patient, and by seeing her daughter as an authentic human being. In doing this, she also recreates herself as a mature human being.

Diana's true guilt has been her free denial of the center both in herself and in her daughter. Her task in life now is to reverse that decision and make a total commitment to the authenticity of the center—in herself and in her daughter.

Diana's Meaning and Importance

In a sense, Diana's child represents her ultimate challenge. All the guilts of her life are focused on her daughter: on her hinges her adequacy as mother, woman, and even the acceptance of the child she once was. But this focus can also be the source of her answer, which will ascribe ultimate meaning to her life. She will know the meaning of being an important and a needed person.

Generalized, the message to all of us is:

1. Find your true guilt.
2. Devote your life to its correction.

When Diana first became able to express her problem in words, her dilemma was completely intertwined with some of the great problems of human existence. After an existential analysis, she understands that these dilemmas are eternal problems without solutions and that they need not be solved in terms of the problems of everyday existence. This makes it easier for her to deal with her day-to-day problems;

she cannot resolve the issue of life and death, but she can choose to say "yes" or "no" to her daughter. The polarities of existence have rendered a choice possible.

The Conservative Reply

Shortly after our class discussion of Diana's letter, I received the following communication from a very conservative middle-aged Catholic woman, also a member of the class.

Dear Dr. Koestenbaum:

I give you the reverse side of the coin: I have just discovered that my eighteen-year-old daughter has been sleeping with her boyfriend!

Though I have not entertained even the thought of committing suicide (as the father in last Tuesday's letter), I have experienced a feeling that must be closely related to death. I reached the depths of depression—I wept—and wept—and wept . . . tears of sadness for my daughter's loss of innocence . . . tears of recrimination at what I consider my own failings.

I have been consumed with guilt. I see in phantasm all the little impatiences—the moments of neglect—the times I have been too busy or too tired to listen when she might have needed me. I have failed her.

As a sociology major, I am cognizant of the latest statistics on virginity—almost 80% of the sample polled do not consider virginity important. So I am an anachronism. But we have raised our children (my husband and I) in a religion that considers sex a privilege of marriage and holds that premarital sex is sinful. Apparently our daughter is rejecting our values. And of course, she has the right and the free will to make her choice.

When we discussed the situation (she and I) I asked her if she loved her boyfriend or if they had plans to marry. She said he loves her, but she does *not know*—this (of course) made me unhappy for I cannot conceive of sex without love and I see the great proliferation of depersonalized sex in our culture as a threat to the human-ness that places man uniquely above the animal kingdom.

Our daughter now wants to move out—she attended one semester of college and quit. She plans to work (she has a part-time job now and is looking further) and then return to school next fall. She does not wish to get married (I agree with her that she is not mature enough for marriage) but she is so vulnerable and the shyest of all [4] of our children. I gave her "Vitality of Death" to read, the passage about the teen-age couple whose sexual attraction was overwhelming. She seems to be following one of your alternatives and is seeing her boyfriend infrequently.

This letter is acting as a catharsis—I feel somewhat less anxious simply from having written it. I'm not sure I want you to read it to the class—young people of today are so sophisticated and experienced that I fear their derision. . . .

Very sincerely,
Mrs. Pamela W.

Mrs. W. has to confront the dreadful possibility that the value system on which her whole life has been based may be wrong. She comes from an age that may be forever past. That possibility leads to the next insight, that her value system stands or falls by her own affirmation of it. As far as she is concerned, her conservative values are true because *she* says—through her life-style—that they are true. They are true exactly as long as she commits her full being to them. That insight is both comforting and frightening; it leads to both peace and vertigo. The metaphysical nature of man confirms her freedom—that is supportive. But the metaphysical nature of man does not give her any value system whatever, and that fact gives her anxiety.

Mrs. W. must learn to lead her own life regardless of her daughter's changes in values. She may have to face the inevitable reality that her daughter will be permanently different from her. That is a consequence of human freedom.

Because of the subjective inwardness (the transcendental ego) of her daughter, which is irreducible, Mrs. W. can do little or nothing to change her daughter's life-style. Her daughter has the independence of all human beings, and meddling is likely to make everything worse.

Furthermore, Mrs. W. must have faith in her daughter and deep respect for the differences between them, according to the principle of individuality. Having faith in her daughter means that she recognizes her daughter's reality. Faith in her daughter is also an expression of love for her. She must think and say, "I am in despair over your way of life. But I fully respect your right to choose for yourself—and I love you for having used that right and chosen freely."

There is then something positive Mrs. W. can do for her daughter: love her, communicate with her, appreciate her, and share with her—including her own motherly feelings of distress. I have observed often that there is little real intimate and loving (that is, existential and authentic) communication between parents and their children until a crisis arises. Then there is something to communicate about!

Finally, Mrs. W. must reaffirm and return to her own religious faith. She must hold on to her own personal integrity. Conservative Catholicism is part of her world-view, and the more intensely she devotes herself to perceive the world through the eyes of her religion the more authentic and fulfilled a person she will be.

7:

A Program
for Self-Development

How can you learn from Diana's insights and apply them to your life? Existential philosophy can help people achieve good mental health. Existential insights must be quickly translated into therapeutic actions. In this chapter I will make some suggestions which are simple, have worked in the past, and are based on the fact that Diana's self-disclosure led her to the meanings of many of the themes of the Master Table.

Let us begin by examining how you can benefit from using the Insight Application Form.

The Insight Application Form

By participating in the activity of philosophical facilitation you experience a certain amount of growth. You must then capitalize on that growth. You have found a little pearl in your shell which you must now cultivate. The following steps from the Insight Application Form are suggestions to consolidate and amplify your growth.

1. You must *understand* what you have achieved. You must conceptualize it, write it down, memorize it, refer to it again and again. You must read about it and write about it. Once conceptualized, the insight has the potential of being permanently rooted in your consciousness. You must be convinced that your participation in this activity has been a genuine act of growth, and that to grow is the nature of man. When you grow you will feel healthy and authentic; when you do not grow you can feel depressed and worthless. You must always look for growth in every one of your daily activities.

2. You must select an ideal *model*. Your self-concept will guide you

through life. If your self-concept is vivid and constant, it will slowly but reliably change you and your world-view. You must be intellectually clear about the existential personality theory so that your life-style will gradually conform to an authentic human existence. This consideration follows from the principle of responsibility ("I have created and am responsible for the organization of my world; I did not create the raw materials, but I am fully and alone responsible for the social reality that I have constructed around me and the life-style that I have organized for myself"). Each person can contribute much to his happiness by keeping constantly before himself and internalizing his ideal self-concept. The child has the parent, hopefully, to serve as model. But each of us can select his own model and retain its image clearly in the mind.

3. You must *verbalize* your insight. That is accomplished by discussing it. You must make a deliberate effort to seek out friends with whom you can discuss the need for growth and ways of growing. Be aware of the individuals with whom you can discuss your need for growth, and what groups and associations exist in which your growth-need can be discussed. On college and high school campuses, on the job and in the churches, there exist innumerable opportunities for extracurricular as well as curricular activities in which kindred minds can meet. An individual who seeks authenticity has the responsibility of creating for himself an environment that supports the particular version of his quest. It is as easy to modify the environment to suit one's needs and tastes as it is difficult to become authentic unaided, on one's own.

4. You must *experience* your insight. You must not only think and talk but also experience. You can experience growth in two ways: by *recollection* and by *practice*. To recollect means to experience vicariously past moments of growth: you must list them and feel your way into them so that they appear new and real. Practice means that you must savor each growth experience to make it as large as possible in your experience of your world. A growth experience is like enjoying good food and good wine; you must make yourself fully aware of the flavor, the texture, and the consistency. Full awareness of each experience of growth will help you consolidate your gains.

5. You must *integrate* and concretize your growth through habit formation and environmental manipulation. For this, you need a program that will intensify your learning. One way Diana can grow is to lose weight. That can be accomplished successfully only with a complete reorganization of her life: she must learn to enjoy each moment of "eating less" or of "hunger," because these are moments of meaningful growth. She might keep a chart of achievements in weight reduction, small but continuous, and savor repeatedly each one of her successes. Furthermore, she must change her environment

to remove temptations. She could enroll in a social program of either exercise or weight-watching. She must be conscious at all times of the fact that she is trying to mold her habits and her environment so as to achieve loss of weight. A good model before her eyes will help.

Mrs. G., who was seventy-six years old, needed to integrate her small philosophic growth into her life-style. She had found work in a suicide prevention bureau. Working there kept her busy, but it was not enough to give her meaning. She had tried many other jobs before. But once she understood that growth is forever, that what matters is the process and not the achievement, her attitude toward her work changed. Before philosophical understanding, she worked to pass the time and to keep busy; her work was thus dull and un-fulfilling. She changed jobs frequently, looking for an activity that would make her into an "object" with which she could be satisfied. After some personalized instruction in philosophy she was able to reinterpret the meaning of her work: now she saw her work as the best way for her to grow; as a meaning-giving and fulfilling process rather than as a dreary and escapist search for a specific achievement.

Diana was asked to complete the Insight Application Form. Her answers follow.

INSIGHT APPLICATION FORM

Name the philosophical insight: The Principle of
Growth: My life is an endless process of growing,
emerging and researching out.

1. Understanding: Explain the insight in detail:
I have expressed my problems and given them to my
teacher. In so doing I have expressed the desire to
grow. That desire is part of man's universal nature
Health means continuous growth. To grow means to
always move into a real future. I shall choose to
always move ahead regardless of difficulties.

2. Model: Name a person (living or dead) that you
would like to be: I choose two: Helen of Troy and
Helen Keller.

Now visualize and record how that person exemplifies
the philosophic insight: Helen of Troy reaches out
to the world through her beauty. I want to be beautiful like her. I want to have the face that laun-
ched a thousand ships. I really believe that if I
think I am her I will become more like her. I have
always admired Helen Keller. She is strong. She
has courage. She never gives up. She conquers all.
Imagining I am Helen Keller gives me the strength
to do the many difficult things that lie ahead. I
enjoy this kind of thinking.

3. Verbalizations: List opportunities for discussing and sharing the philosophical insight:

(1) I will make an appointment with Rev. S   and
discuss youth groups.

(2) I will write a letter to Jane B., who has not
heard from me for three years and tell her where I
am in life.

(3) I will read a child's story about growth to my daughter.

(4)

4. Experiences: A. Recollections: List past moments in which the above philosophical insight was experience: (1) I experienced growth when I had my baby

(2) I experienced growth when Mrs. A., my math teacher, told me I was her best student.

(3) I experienced growth when I summoned my courage to break up with my boyfriend Tom.

(4) I experienced growth when I finally decided to move to a new apartment in a more quiet neighborhood.

B. Practice. Suggest possible experiences today:
 (1) I will cancel the date for this weekend I made with Bill. I did not want to make that date in the first place.

(2) I will today make a much overdue appointment with the dentist.

(3) I will start to read today Tellich's "The Courage to Be."

(4)

5. Integration: List a program of five steps which will maximize good habits, including a realistic reorganization of your life:

(1) I will seek psychological counseling. This begins with the search for references.

(2) I will find a physician and consult with him about losing weight.

(3) I will speak to my teachers about improving my grades and clearing past incomplete courses.

(4) I will join a weight watchers organization. I will first find a list of possible ones in the telephone directory.

(5) I will swim three days a week.

Exercise

Select an insight that seems real to you. Write it down on the Insight Application Form below. Now develop a program for self-improvement and philosophic growth toward health by filling in the blanks of your form. The task may seem minor and somewhat pedantic; nevertheless, growth occurs in small and manageable stages rather than in grand transformations.

Let us continue the program for self-development by discussing a journal that I frequently ask my private students to keep.

INSIGHT APPLICATION FORM

Name the philosophical insight: _____

_____

1. *Understanding:* Explain the insight in detail: _____

_____

_____

_____

_____

_____

2. *Model:* Name a person (living or dead) that you would like to be: _____

_____

Now visualize and record how that person exemplifies the philosophic insight: _____

_____

_____

_____

_____

_____

_____

_____

3. *Verbalizations:* List opportunities for discussing and sharing the philosophical insight: (1)_____

_____

    (2)_____

_____

    (3)_____

_____

    (4)_____

_____

4. *Experiences:*

A. Recollections: List past moments in which the above philosophical insight was experienced: (1) _____

(2) _____

(3) _____

(4) _____

B. *Practice.* Suggest possible experiences today:
(1) _____

(2) _____

(3) _____
(4) _____

5. *Integration:* List a program of 5 steps which will maximize good habits, including a realistic reorganization of your life: (1) _____

(2) _____

(3) _____

(4) _____

(5) _____

8:

The Journal

All of us must learn to like and appreciate ourselves. What practical steps can we take to achieve that? We must develop an answer—a prescription or treatment.

The E-I-F Journal:
Understanding and Experiencing

If you are truly interested in a philosophical reconstruction of your life, you will greatly benefit from keeping an intellectual journal or emotional diary. The journal must contain three types of material—all honest. It must include *emotional* (E), *intellectual* or *conceptual* (I), and *fantasy* (F) material.

In order to write this kind of journal, you must first learn how to write. What, specifically, is journal-writing? It is the ability to *become* the writing. The journal writer must learn to write fast, to *narrow* the space between the fantasy, thought, or feeling and the written word. He will soon be able to think writing or write thinking. Journal-writing is not communication; it is *expression* or *being*. You *are* your writing. In this journal you will work out your destiny. If you are religious, you can view it as a written prayer and you can address it to God, with the understanding that only you and God will know its contents. You may address it to mother or father, or to some other significant person in your life. You may address it to an imaginary or invented person, or to yourself or parts of yourself (such as your rational aspect or your unconscious). The only rule is that it must be both explicit and honest. It must open the floodgates of your inwardness and release its contents for you to see.

You must not throw away the journal, but you need not reread it. Use whatever freedom you have to organize your life in such a way that there will be daily time for your journal. It does not matter that you have extensive entries—what does matter is that you make entries daily. Finally, the journal is not a record of behavior and events but an expression of your emotional and human development. It is *growth* achieved through the written word, and the written word flows like the time that you are (principle C 12).

Here is a sample (unedited) from an E-I-F journal shown to me by Bill, one of my students. Bill is nineteen, very bright, rather immature, and a college sophomore. He writes only to be himself honestly, not for effect or communication. In order to facilitate the production of material, I gave him the following assignment: record your (a) fantasies, (b) dreams, (c) ideal self, and (d) real self.

My fantasies are taking over my life. I wonder what it means. Today I plan to record my fantasies and my dreams. I am glad I am writing this journal but must keep it private—at least for a while.

I am going to list my fantasies:

1. I like to think that I am destined to be a profound thinker, a significant contributer to knowledge or art.

2. I wish I had started playing guitar at age 10 instead of age 18. Perhaps I would be a folksinger, a wandering poet, a lonely searching artist.

3. I have often want to be a frog-prince capable of any mixture of frogly and human characteristics. I think a human size and intellect would be best with a frog body. As a giant size frog I would make love to a gypsy princess in back of a gondola. It would be beautiful. Wouldn't you like to make love to a giant frog?

4. I sometimes wish that a war would come and I was among the survivors, then I would work hard to make us all happy in such hard times. Then people would know that I love them. I could prove it to them.

5. To have an independent source of income, an inheritance or something enough to last for the rest of my life. That way I would not have to worry about working. I could travel, write poems, go fishing, paint pictures, make love and fly kites with little kids.

Here are additional and compulsive-like fantasies, desires:

1. I often have urges to caress and kiss perfect strangers, to make love to objects (i.e. trees, cars, rocks).

2. I often have urges to break bottles or glasses, to shatter everything into little pieces.

I am now going to record my dreams:

1. I put up a holy brazen plaque to keep out demons, but while I am sleeping the demon comes anyway. I awake and defend myself with my trusty Swiss army pocketknife. I flee to the backyard where there are snakes drown in mudholes. There are crippled lizards and legless bleeding frogs. Gawking geese guard the only exit to the cobblestone streets of the peaceful town where all are happy.

(A cork on the bottle, a mute on the trumpet).

2. There was a girl who was a cartoon artist. I fell in love with her. Her comic-book fantasies swept me away. I had just moved into an old house where a dying chinaman lived.

The cartoonist girl and I went to the county fair. There was a tough-guy there who bumped into me and spilt his coffee. He got mad and asked me (told me) to pay for his coffee. He had been loosing his collection of half-dollars through a whole in his pants pocket all day, so when the coffee accident happened he was *really* mad.

This tough guy didn't like the old chinaman either. He wanted the old man to die and get it over with so he wouldn't have to look at that sick old face anymore.

I moved out of that house where the chinaman lived and sent to look for the cartoonist girl who I'd lost at the fair.

The following is my Ideal Self:

Tall, slim, healthy, with dark hair. A man who quietly watches his active movements in the world. A man who is aware the subtle beauty in the hussle-bussle of the everchanging world. A man who can pause to enjoy all the gentle oranges at the corner fruit stand in the sun. A family man with an active career a lovely wife, and 3 kids. I must never stop growing never stop learning.

This is my Real Self:

I am skinny, a little too weak. I must move my thoughts outwards more towards others. I find it hard to care for those I do not respect. I only disrespect them because I am repressing a part of myself which is very much like them. I dislike them because I dislike part of myself.

I want to give, but am afraid of being rejected. I don't really see why; in a sense all of us are already rejected. Christ was rejected more than most.

Love is a simple thing. It is only fear that makes it difficult, fear of losing something, fear of losing myself. But those things that I *can* lose are *not* myself.

Anything that is changeable is not really me. I am that power which is able to make change, that power which can lose things (my hair, my job, my reputation, my friends, my personality) and still survive.

I do not know myself very well. I am hidden beneath, behind and amongst a huge mass of "things."

Loving and Being Loved

Bill has now become visible: He has expressed—laid out before him —his true nature, for his own self-discovery. He has done it by listing fantasies and dreams and by describing his ideal and his real self.

Let us now return to Diana and follow her program for philosophic reconstruction. By emulating her you can gain pointers on how to use the E-I-F journal for your own personal growth, development, and search for meaning. In addition to wanting self-expression she, like all of us, desperately needs to love and be loved. To make that possible, she must use her journal to understand the concept of love and encounter. That can be achieved through the fantasy part of her journal. She can help herself develop this understanding through reading, courses, and through constant writing on the subject. In this way she can even help herself in the absence of another person who loves her.

Love is not just an experience; it is also the understanding of the nature of man and his possibilities. Love is learned conceptually as well as experientially. Again, Diana must use the limited freedom still available to her to give herself an adequate reading list or a sufficient intellectual education on the nature and meaning of love. Because available and relevant books change from time to time and from person to person, it is difficult to give an all-purpose list here. Suggestions that were useful to Diana included Erich Fromm's *The Art of Loving* and Ernesto Cardenal's *To Live Is to Love*.

How can an existential phenomenology help you, as it helped Diana, understand the meaning of love? Here are some suggestions.

To understand the concept of existential encounter and existential love you must understand the difference between, on the one hand, your consciousness, your awareness, your inward and subjective self, your ultimate center, and, on the other hand, your behavior, your personality, your roles, the games you play, and your body. Remember principle A 2: "I am a pure consciousness that has a psychological personality, a physical body, and many social roles."

You are that subjective consciousness. The religious person discovers that inward consciousness in his relation with God. The non-religious person discovers it in searching for the inmost depth of his soul and finds it in his readiness to die and his capacity to give up everything. That is the concept of the first, inner, or transcendental self. We are now ready to define existential love, which is the same as an existential encounter.

An existential encounter is the ability to recognize the consciousness that I am through recognizing the sacred integrity of the consciousness that you are. That relation between two pure consciousnesses I call a transcendental relationship. It can be described as follows, in keeping with the principle of love ("As an adult I can choose to love him and care for him"):

"You are my limit; my land ends where your land begins. Your needs limit my needs. When I recognize in truth and clarity the beautiful and absolute fullness of your existence then I become your limit. I see that your land ends where mine begins and my needs thus limit your needs. You have become a mirror to me and through the purity of that mirror I, for the first time perhaps, discover my own center.

"I can now choose to care for your center; I can choose freely to make a commitment to your center."

Love is thus both a discovery (the mirror) and a decision (the choice of caring). You are now in a position to conceptualize encounter. Let us turn once more to Diana.

Encounter, Asceticism, and Forgiveness

Diana has successfully conceptualized the meaning of love as encounter. But she is still alone. Following is an exercise that will help her experience love and assist her in moving out of herself in order to both give and find love. In other words, Diana must *experience* the concept of encounter in order to really understand and then apply it. There are really several exercises that can help her experience the existence of her inward consciousness. First, she must experiment with total *asceticism* (either literally or in fantasy, the latter usually being sufficient) to discover and experience *her own inner self*. Second, she must experiment with total *forgiveness* in order to experience the reality of *another* pure consciousness. Understanding and being able to imagine a relationship with people on that basic level will give her the idea and the experience of the inner nature of man and the real foundation for an authentic encounter relationship.

What is asceticism? It is total denial of the body and the personality. It is the discovery of the silent mind within. Eastern mystics and Western saints have made asceticism a style of life and a cultural desideratum. But for Diana, asceticism was a fantasy exercise only— a guided daydream. Let us follow Diana through her daydream.

Diana first did some exercises for relaxation. I asked her to alternately flex and relax, region by region, all the muscles of her body, beginning with her feet and ending with her facial and head muscles. I then suggested to her that she feel warm and glowing all over and then that she feel her heavy weight massively leaning against the surface on which she was resting.

Here is an abbreviated transcription of her *asceticism fantasy*. She spoke every word out loud and made sure that she heard it and that she truly meant what she was saying.

> I am hungry. I feel my hunger in my stomach. My stomach hurts; my mouth waters. I want to place a soft candy bar in my mouth and chew it and swallow it.
>
> The hunger is not me. I am not the hunger. The wish to eat is not me; I am not the wish to eat. The hunger is a distant object in the world, like a star in the heavens, like a nest high upon a tree. I am not a hungry self but a self that perceives hunger as some distant thing. The hunger is not me but I can touch the hunger with a long stick.
>
> That pure, empty, silent and observing self is my true inwardness.
>
> I have a bad sore in my mouth. The sore hurts badly; it is getting worse. The sore appears to be closer to my center than my stomach hunger because my mouth is closer to the real "me" than is my stomach. I seem to be centered inside the top of my head, between the eyes. The sore is closer to my center. I am forcing myslf not to give a damn about the sore. I don't care if it hurts. I don't care if it gets worse. In fact, I make it hurt by poking it with my finger to practice detachment from it. I don't care if my whole head gets infected, tender, and I die. I really don't care! The sore prevents me from living effectively, but I no longer care about living. I am really able to give up everything! A strange sensation! A freeing experience! A peaceful moment!
>
> The self that gives up life itself and the world with it is my true subjective inwardness, my pure consciousness, my transcendental self.
>
> I want sex. My pelvic region seems to be closer to me than my stomach, since I am sometimes centered in my pelvis. I am sometimes in the eyes and sometimes in the pelvis. Now my center is in the pelvis from which all living movement radiates in waves.
>
> I am now giving up even sex. I am at this moment taking the vow of celibacy. Sex now becomes a distant desire. In fact, desire itself is a thing in the distance; it is no longer me. Desire exists, I perceive it, but is no longer me. I exist at a big distance from even the desires of my pelvis.
>
> That distant self is my true inwardness, my pure consciousness. I've discovered it; I am it; I feel it!

Diana has now made significant progress toward actually experiencing her own true inwardness. It is this part of her that must be recognized by herself and by others as the true Diana.

Her next task is to recognize that pure conscious inwardness in *others*. Then the idea of a transcendental communication or true encounter will finally be accurately understood by her. That is true because encounter is the meeting of two consciousnesses.

Following is a summary and an edited version of Diana's *forgiveness-fantasy:*

> I see a man; I have decided that I want to perceive him not as a body but as another subjective consciousness just like my own. I don't want to see him as a body or as a personality; nor do I wish to see him as being his roles or his physical appearance. I want to see him only as a subjective inwardness. I, therefore, make him ugly in my fantasy. He is ugly everywhere: in the face, the hands, his torso, and his legs. Furthermore, he is dirty, smelly, and generally disgusting. But for all of this I forgive him. I make the religious decision to love him. In forgiving him I perceive the self behind the ugliness and the dirt, and that is his true inward self, precisely like mine. I speak to that self. I say, "Hello, I forgive you and I love you!"
>
> The fantasy gets worse. The man is not only ugly but also evil. His body is evil and so is his behavior and personality. He is a mean and vicious criminal. He has done horrible things that deserve only death. In fact, I vomit at the very thought of his evil deeds.
>
> Nevertheless, I shout, "I forgive you!" Behind that atrocious behavior exists the purest self, a center, an inward consciousness cursed with an evil personality. The center is as unaffected by the evil that surrounds it as a rainbow is unaffected by the torrential waterfall over which it hovers. I address myself to that center and say softly this time: "Hello! I forgive you because I love you."
>
> I now experience the true inwardness behind the evil person. That is why I do not believe in the death penalty for even the most heinous criminal. I am able to love the consciousness behind the criminal.
>
> I now perceive a pure ego and through that perception I recognize my own pure ego.

She later recorded both fantasies in her E-I-F journal.

The ascetic forgiving the criminal—that is the paradigm for a transcendental human relationship. Diana has experienced it through fantasy, and her conceptual understanding has thus been increased. She now understands the concept of encounter and the notion of an authentic—i.e., transcendental—relationship.

There is an even more profound and accurate mode of perceiving the structure of the pure ascetic consciousness that is your home: it is the intuition of the silent consciousness or the consciousness of silence. Silence is not only the absence of noise but also the absence of sights, and above all, the absence of thoughts and ideas. The pure consciousness that you are is total silence and total emptiness. That with which you are in touch when you think of nothing at all is your pure consciousness. That emptiness is accessible to all who are willing to practice meditation. Meditation is most effective when one focuses on nothing at all at moments when it seems least likely or most difficult, such as at times of great excitement or grave pain.

In actual life, Diana had never experienced that kind of a meeting—that is, an encounter of consciousnesses. Her meetings were always bodily. To meet a man meant for Diana to thrust her body on him, or to thrust her role as the "eternal feminine being" on him. Similarly, she expected men to meet her as a body, to perceive her as a body. Her value was her body. To conceive of and experience a transcendental relationship—an existential encounter, a consciousness-to-consciousness meeting—was totally new for her. In short, love was new to her. Love means acceptance and recognition, devotion and care, not performance. Knowledge of the nature of love was one of the most important messages that philosophy could bring to Diana.

Through her obesity, Diana was saying, in effect, "All male-female relationships are physical. I've tried and tried but found no satisfaction. I now make myself unattractive, because the physical encounter is not the real me. But I cannot substitute anything for it, because I do not understand the pure conscious inwardness that I am." In short, Diana needs philosophic (existential phenomenological) education—conceptually and emotionally. She needs to understand and experience her own consciousness and the relationship between consciousnesses.

Existential Integration

You now know the intellectual and the emotional meaning of the concept of love or transcendental encounter, and should be able to understand it through experience. Your major task remains: *express* it now by fully integrating it into your real life.

Diana's next step is to understand how she has failed that model of love in her life. In the past she has not been able to live the idea of a centered self. A centered self is able to love and be loved, and if she has failed in love it is because her center did not exist. Her principal task, therefore, is to build authentic relationships, from her center to that of another. Following are simple and straightforward suggestions for anyone who has difficulty integrating his knowledge and understanding with his real life.

First, *learn how to build on your already existing strengths.* Do not look for new relationships; rather, strengthen those that are already available. Who are the significant persons in Diana's life? Her daughter, a friend or two, a neighbor, etc. Diana can begin her program for authenticity by loving her daughter and understanding her real needs and by learning in this way to love girlhood and childhood in general.

Meaning and love can be reclaimed most deeply by devotion to a child. This is illustrated in the E-I-F journal of Mary Lou. By rekindling her love for her son, she built on her already existing strengths.

Mary Lou is twenty-three, and has a three-year-old boy, Ian. She is jealous of her husband, who spends much time away from home with his profession as an art teacher.

The following is an excerpt from a letter from Mary Lou:

> I wonder most of all about your relationship with your wife. I wonder this because I am a wife whose husband has another love, and you are a husband who has another love. Your love is for philosophy, my husband's love is for art. I feel something like jealousy of you and of my husband because you have found something so important, so all involving, so much of life. I feel a deep insecurity because I have not found this. I feel a deep fear because I don't believe there is any more for me. I wonder how your wife feels. Perhaps she is not the insecure person that I am, but surely she faces similar problems. What does she do when you are gone nights in a row lecturing, writing, meetings, etc. . . ? Does she have something that is just hers, or has she given you all her interest? Has she taken a deep interest in your work, does she like and understand your love of philosophy? I don't really know what I want to know except maybe that there might be people who never find more. For myself, I am not satisfied through my husband's art, and I have not found that something else that's just mine. And I really fear that I won't find it. I am very dissatisfied with myself.

My recommendation to Mary Lou was to seek meaning in her son. She was close to the moment that Tillich called *kairos* (crisis), so that my suggestion properly impressed her as the right solution. She wrote in her journal of her new-found time to be spent with Ian and her renewed devotion for him. The statement and analysis of each one of their new activities together was preceded in her journal by an appropriate photograph. The captions were: "At the Park," "At the Zoo," "Bicycling in the Woods," etc. Her last picture touched me deeply: Mary Lou and Ian waving goodbye at me into the camera.

Mary Lou titles this section of her journal, "My Exercise in Living." Her journal is

a free expression of my exercise in living as experienced since the encounter group meeting with Dr. Koestenbaum. At that time I made the decision to live my life by accepting it as the life I have chosen for myself, and also as the best possible life. This has been a very conscious and deliberate decision that has been renewed many times each day. It has not always been a successful decision because I find too little psychical distance between my empirical ego and my consciousness. But the decision is an exercise in living because when it is successful I find great inner peace, and by consciously making the decision to reconstruct my outlook on life each day, in time I hope to be able to make the decision unconsciously, thus having reconstructed my intentionality of consciousness.

Part of the exercise is to relive my childhood through my son, Ian. Together we have learned a great deal in the last several months. It has felt good to be actively involved in play and to return to the joys of childhood. The activity in itself is physically exhausting, but I find myself rejuvenated after our most wild romps. I feel a closeness to him, but also I feel very much in touch with myself.

RIDING AT STANFORD

I woke up saddened on this particular day because my husband had to work, and would not be able to spend the day with Ian and I. I found myself becoming depressed about the lack of time we have together. This is when I made the decision to pack the bike and take a long bike ride with Ian. Besides learning that travel is a symbol for space and time, I have felt the experience of this movement in time. By riding a great distance it is impossible to stay in a depression. It seems that a depression is standing still, is being stagnated, while movement is growth. Although I become very physically tired after riding a great distance, I feel more mentally awake, more rejuvenated, and my physical tiredness feels good. I have known the tiredness and boredom of mental anguish and depression and it feels bad for there is no reason for it. Whenever I feel depression coming on now, I choose to be physically active.

As we rode, I returned to very basic feelings. Ian sang to me, and I felt lucky to have a beautiful child with me. I felt the beauty in the breeze that was cooling me, and in the sounds of the twittering birds. I concentrated on pedaling and on the rhythm of my breathing. I thought of my destination, and the pedaling became easier. Soon it became almost unconscious as if someone else were doing it. This is probably the closest I have come to separation my consciousness and my empirical ego. I felt that I was distant from my body, looking down on myself as if I were not involved in what I was doing.

A later entry reads as follows:

As I watch Ian play on this particular day I find myself feeling a great joy in him. As he climbs the slide he looks to me for approval, and I also feel a great responsibility for him. As I am reconstructing my life I am helping to constitute his, and I now feel that I am doing the best for him I can. I still feel a great inconsistency in dealing with him, but I feel secure even in this inconsistency. It seems that I am learning to accept such inconsistencies as a natural part of life. I understand now what you meant when you said to me that my meaning in life will be found through Ian. While watching him I feel the absolute necessity to respect myself as a person, as a woman, as a wife and as a mother. I feel the need to feel secure in my center. In so finding my center I will be better able to teach Ian this basic love for the humanity of all man, and better able to share love and understanding with Paul, my husband.

And later:

I feel that I have been more understanding of him [my husband, Paul] since my decision to accept my life, for it was also a decision to accept the relationship we have in marriage as meaningful and good. Since the decision to accept, I find that things somehow have changed for the better. I cannot say exactly what that change is except that possibly it is one of viewing the relationship in a completely different light. At any rate, my exercise in living has in no way excluded Paul even though he has not been with Ian and I on most of our outings. Each time I have gone home with a new "look of love" at the world, at Ian, at Paul, and most of all at myself!

Mary Lou has built on her strengths. Like Diana, she discovered conceptually what an authentic (that is, loving) human relationship demands. Then she integrated that knowledge with her life by building on her already existing strengths: her relationships to her husband and her son. Her success was immediate. Let us now turn to a further recommendation on how to translate insight to real living.

A second suggestion for existential integration is to *learn to identify mature, self-actualizing, and authentic individuals and then relate to them deliberately.* Find out, also, to the best of your ability, why you may not have been able to do this in the past.

For Diana, previous relationships consisted primarily in using people or in being used. She had two male friends, Jack and Robert. Jack used Diana for sexual purposes only, whereas Robert needed someone for whom he could have contempt and whom he could criticize. Diana willingly lent herself to both of these neurotic purposes. Her real need was for warm and accepting friends, but her reality was cold, cynical, and indifferent. After some philosophic growth, however, she is now alert to her tendency toward inauthentic relationships. She catches herself every time she drifts into a "business" rather than a "personal" relationship.

A third suggestion is to *congregate or live in mature environments.* Avoid circumstances that are likely to yield inauthentic people, as in a bar, with a neurotic roommate, within a depressing neighborhood or a squelching job. You can even purchase mature environments—schools and psychotherapy. A therapeutic relationship should be, in many respects, a model human relationship. A therapist calls this mode of integration environmental manipulation.

Finally, integration means to *be honest in relationships,* especially between the sexes. Honesty leads directly to a transcendental relationship, a relationship of one pure consciousness with another. Honesty can be used as a technical device to help two people relate as inward and subjective consciousnesses—in the spirit of true love, care, and mutual understanding and acceptance rather than merely as two bodies, as in mechanical sex, or two roles, as in a business transaction. In a relationship that demands and tolerates honesty, the basic person is what counts rather than his superficial accomplishments or visible attributes.

Honest relationships are realistic relationships: no promises are made, even by innuendo, that cannot be kept, and a relationship is maintained only as long as it can be meaningful. In honest relationships an individual is his true self; he plays no games.

Ellen

Let us consider an example of this honesty in a male-female relationship. Ellen, twenty-eight, an unmarried schoolteacher, is having an affair with a forty-five-year-old man, John, who is married and has three children. John is aggressive, irascible, and a good sexual partner; he drinks excessively, has a very dependent wife, and a life-long history of affairs. Ellen is confused and unhappy because she is totally involved with John: her life is focused on him, while her future with him is uncertain at best. How would honesty help Ellen?

Honesty points in two directions: you and me. First, Ellen must be honest with herself. She perceives John as filling something like 90 percent of her total life picture, when in reality he can at best occupy only 15 percent of it.

If she is honest, she will admit to herself that John is not available as a future husband, and that he is not accessible even as a good, loyal, and mature friend. He is accessible to Ellen only as a sexual object and a passing companion. If she sees him as 90 percent of her world, she is dishonest with herself; if she sees him as 15 percent of her total world, she is honest. (It would also be dishonest to see him as 0 percent of her world, for she cannot give him up.) So much for honesty with herself.

Honesty with John is another matter. She thought it her duty to be 100 percent honest with John, but total honesty with him is in this case impossible. Partial honesty may be indicated but is not essential. Because John is 15 percent of her world, she owes him exactly this percentage of honesty or sharing. In other words, by being fully honest with John she was really being dishonest with herself, pretending he was something he was not. What Ellen does need desperately, however, is to establish an honest relationship with a man who can and will reciprocate. She needs a 100 percent relationship.

In simple English, Ellen needs a friend first and a sexual partner second. She has a history of meeting men superficially and sexually. Her first value is sexual. Later, after sex, she tries openess—which then fails. I suggested to her she do the reverse, telling her that she has not yet met the man she wants to marry because she has had no experience or practice in meeting men on an honest, open, and mature person-to-person, rather than body-to-body level. She must start relationships with honest confrontation and open meeting. Once a transcendental connection has been established, she can take the sexual initiative herself if necessary. An authentic woman attracts the man she wants through her authenticity, not through her body and her sexual competence.

Honesty cannot be achieved with the immature, because a person must first be honest with himself before honesty with a lover makes any sense. The corollary of this insight is that love is not for children but for adults—and adulthood is more likely to begin in the middle thirties than in the teens!

Exercises

The following activities will help you gain further benefits from this chapter.

1. Select the three themes from the Master Table that are the most relevant to your life.

2. Develop an Insight Application Form for each of these themes.

3. Start an E-I-F journal.

4. After you have made some progress with these exercises, begin formulating in your journal a program for the *integration* of your insights, as was done by Mary Lou.

Remember that your self-disclosure is of two kinds: individual and philosophical (theme B of the Master Table). Therefore, your integration must not be limited to the psychological insights you may have about your personality structure, but must extend to the philosophic insights that apply to all human beings. Remember also that many of your problems are due to the fact that you are a human being and not due to an illness that afflicts only selected persons.

5. As a corollary to no. 4 above, answer specifically these questions, by discussing them in your E-I-F journal:

a. How can I build on my strengths?

b. Whom do I know who is authentic? How can I relate to him (her, them)?

c. Is my environment mature? If not, how can I change it?

d. Am I honest with myself? With others? How can I improve in being honest?

9:

The Pain Test

In Part One we discussed the general outlines of an existential personality theory as it follows from a development of the concept of consciousness. Several applications were suggested primarily to show the usefulness of the theory for personal development, but also to illustrate the proper nature of that theory of consciousness.

In Part Two we undertake an extensive application of that theory for the understanding and management of pain in many of its forms. By pain I do not mean physical suffering alone. I use the word "pain" to stand for the generalized experience of negation or negativity in life—from anxiety to guilt and from depression to bodily pain.

The Pain Test will provide a measure of how much negation you experience in your life as compared to negation that others experience. In addition, the test discriminates among eight different types of pain. By taking the test you can develop a kind of personal "pain-" or "negation-profile" in terms of which the subsequent discussion will make more sense. The test will also provide you with clues on how to fit the suggestions of Part Two to your own particular personality structure.

Test Yourself: Where Does It Hurt and How Does It Hurt?

What is your "pain mass" and your "pain profile"? This test, like all the others in this book, is not a psychological instrument, strictly speaking. It is simply an exercise to aid your self-understanding and stimulate philosophical discussion.

Here is a list of 285 adjectives. If you do not know the meaning of a word, look it up in a dictionary. Work fast. Decide for each adjective whether it *describes you* at this moment (T or +), or whether it *does not describe you* at this moment (F or o). Then use the following sheets to get your totals.

1. accepted——
2. accomplished——
3. achieving——
4. aching——
5. adult——
6. affectionate——
7. afraid——
8. aggravated——
9. aggressive——
10. agitated——
11. aimless——
12. alienated——
13. alive——
14. alone——
15. ambiguous——
16. ambivalent——
17. angry——
18. annoyed——
19. anxious——
20. appreciated——
21. arthritic——
22. ashamed——
23. asinine——
24. atrophied——
25. attractive——
26. authentic——
27. awed——
28. awful——
29. bad——
30. bitter——
31. blue——
32. bored——
33. bouncy——
34. breathless——
35. bright——
36. broken——
37. burning——
38. callous——
39. capable——
40. choking——
41. comfortable——
42. confident——
43. conflicting——
44. confused——
45. contemptible——
46. contradictory——
47. cramped——
48. creative——
49. crippled——
50. crucified——
51. cruel——

52. crying——
53. dead——
54. defeated——
55. defective——
56. deficient——
57. depressed——
58. desirable——
59. desperate——
60. destroyed——
61. destructive——
62. different——
63. difficult——
64. diffident——
65. dignified——
66. disappointed——
67. discouraged——
68. disgusted——
69. disinterested——
70. distant——
71. dizzy——
72. dreadful——
73. dry——
74. dull——
75. dying——
76. ecstatic——
77. embarrassed——
78. embittered——
79. emphatic——
80. empty——
81. esteemed——
82. evil——
83. exhausted——
84. exuberant——
85. fabulous——
86. failing——
87. fantastic——
88. feeble——
89. fenced in——
90. feverish——
91. foolish——
92. foreign——
93. fragmented——
94. free——
95. frenzied——
96. friendly——
97. frustrated——
98. furious——
99. gleeful—
100. good——
101. grounded——
102. growing——

103. grown-up——
104. guilty——
105. handcuffed——
106. handsome——
107. happy——
108. hard——
109. hateful——
110. hating——
111. healthy——
112. helpless——
113. hemmed in——
114. hindered——
115. hollow——
116. homeless——
117. hostile——
118. humorless——
119. hungry——
120. idiotic——
121. ill——
122. imbecilic——
123. immature——
124. impassive——
125. impeded——
126. imprisoned——
127. inadequate——
128. inappropriate——
129. inauthentic——
130. inconsequential——
131. incredible——
132. independent——
133. indifferent——
134. individual——
135. ineffective——
136. ineffectual——
137. inexperienced——
138. insane——
139. inspired——
140. insubstantial——
141. intelligent——
142. irreplaceable——
143. isolated——
144. itchy——
145. jailed——
146. joyful——
147. judged——
148. jumpy——
149. kind——
150. liked——
151. limited——
152. lonely——
153. lost——

154. loved——
155. loving——
156. low——
157. mad——
158. mature——
159. mean——
160. meaningless——
161. mistaken——
162. murderous——
163. nauseous——
164. negative——
165. nervous——
166. non-existent——
167. nonsensical——
168. odd——
169. out-of-place——
170. pained——
171. painful——
172. panicked——
173. paradoxical——
174. paralyzed——
175. passionate——
176. pathetic——
177. peaceful——
178. petrified——
179. philosophical——
180. pleasant——
181. pleased——
182. pointless——
183. positive——
184. punished——
185. purposeful——
186. purposeless——
187. rebellious——
188. recognized——
189. rejected——
190. relaxed——
191. removed——
192. respected——
193. restricted——
194. rewarded——
195. rheumatoid——
196. ridiculous——
197. rooted——

198. rude——
199. sad——
200. sadistic——
201. safe——
202. sane——
203. screaming——
204. self-actualizing——
205. self-conscious——
206. self-pitying——
207. self-reliant——
208. separated——
209. sexless——
210. sexy——
211. shaken——
212. shameful——
213. shy——
214. sick——
215. sinful——
216. sleepy——
217. slowed down——
218. smart——
219. smiling——
220. sore——
221. sorrowful——
222. spent——
223. split——
224. stagnant——
225. stoical——
226. stopped——
227. strong——
228. stupid——
229. successful——
230. suffocating——
231. suicidal——
232. supported——
233. taut——
234. tender——
235. tense——
236. terrified——
237. thirsty——
238. tight——
239. tired——
240. tolerant——
241. torn——

242. tragic——
243. twisted——
244. ugly——
245. ulcerated——
246. unappreciated——
247. unattached——
248. unattractive——
249. unbelievable——
250. unclear——
251. unconcerned——
252. uncreative——
253. undecided——
254. undeserving——
255. undesirable——
256. unfair——
257. unfeeling——
258. unfree——
259. unimaginative——
260. unique——
261. unjust——
262. unkind——
263. unloved——
264. unreal——
265. unresolved——
266. unspirited——
267. unworthy——
268. uprooted——
269. vacuous——
270. valueless——
271. vanished——
272. vibrant——
273. vicious——
274. vigorous——
275. vile——
276. violent——
277. warm——
278. weak——
279. weakened——
280. weeping——
281. whole——
282. worthless——
283. wrenched——
284. wrong——
285. youthful——

Pain Test Score Sheet (Total Score)

The "correct" answers for *all items* of the Pain Test follow.

Place a check (√) after each correct answer.

1 F O ——	45 T + ——	89 T + ——	133 T + ——
2 F O ——	46 T + ——	90 T + ——	134 F O ——
3 F O ——	47 T + ——	91 T + ——	135 T + ——
4 T + ——	48 F O ——	92 T + ——	136 T + ——
5 F O ——	49 T + ——	93 T + ——	137 T + ——
6 F O ——	50 T + ——	94 F O ——	138 T + ——
7 T + ——	51 T + ——	95 T + ——	139 F O ——
8 T + ——	52 T + ——	96 F O ——	140 T + ——
9 T + ——	53 T + ——	97 T + ——	141 F O ——
10 T + ——	54 T + ——	98 T + ——	142 F O ——
11 T + ——	55 T + ——	99 F O ——	143 T + ——
12 T + ——	56 T + ——	100 F O ——	144 T + ——
13 F O ——	57 T + ——	101 F O ——	145 T + ——
14 T + ——	58 F O ——	102 F O ——	146 F O ——
15 T + ——	59 T + ——	103 F O ——	147 T + ——
16 T + ——	60 T + ——	104 T + ——	148 T + ——
17 T + ——	61 T + ——	105 T + ——	149 F O ——
18 T + ——	62 T + ——	106 F O ——	150 F O ——
19 T + ——	63 T + ——	107 F O ——	151 T + ——
20 F O ——	64 T + ——	108 T + ——	152 T + ——
21 T + ——	65 F O ——	109 T + ——	153 T + ——
22 T + ——	66 T + ——	110 T + ——	154 F O ——
23 T + ——	67 T + ——	111 F O ——	155 F O ——
24 T + ——	68 T + ——	112 T + ——	156 T + ——
25 F O ——	69 T + ——	113 T + ——	157 T + ——
26 F O ——	70 T + ——	114 T + ——	158 F O ——
27 T + ——	71 T + ——	115 T + ——	159 T + ——
28 T + ——	72 T + ——	116 T + ——	160 T + ——
29 T + ——	73 T + ——	117 T + ——	161 T + ——
30 T + ——	74 T + ——	118 T + ——	162 T + ——
31 T + ——	75 T + ——	119 T + ——	163 T + ——
32 T + ——	76 F O ——	120 T + ——	164 T + ——
33 F O ——	77 T + ——	121 T + ——	165 T + ——
34 T + ——	78 T + ——	122 T + ——	166 T + ——
35 F O ——	79 F O ——	123 T + ——	167 T + ——
36 T + ——	80 T + ——	124 T + ——	168 T + ——
37 T + ——	81 F O ——	125 T + ——	169 T + ——
38 T + ——	82 T + ——	126 T + ——	170 T + ——
39 F O ——	83 T + ——	127 T + ——	171 T + ——
40 T + ——	84 F O ——	128 T + ——	172 T + ——
41 F O ——	85 F O ——	129 T + ——	173 T + ——
42 F O ——	86 T + ——	130 T + ——	174 T + ——
43 T + ——	87 F O ——	131 F O ——	175 F O ——
44 T + ——	88 T + ——	132 F O ——	176 T + ——

177 F O ———	214 T + ———	251 T + ———
178 T + ———	215 T + ———	252 T + ———
179 T + ———	216 T + ———	253 T + ———
180 F O ———	217 T + ———	254 T + ———
181 F O ———	218 F O ———	255 T + ———
182 T + ———	219 F O ———	256 T + ———
183 F O ———	220 T + ———	257 T + ———
184 T + ———	221 T + ———	258 T + ———
185 F O ———	222 T + ———	259 T + ———
186 T + ———	223 T + ———	260 F O ———
187 T + ———	224 T + ———	261 T + ———
188 F O ———	225 T + ———	262 T + ———
189 T + ———	226 T + ———	263 T + ———
190 F O ———	227 F O ———	264 T + ———
191 T + ———	228 T + ———	265 T + ———
192 F O ———	229 F O ———	266 T + ———
193 T + ———	230 T + ———	267 T + ———
194 F O ———	231 T + ———	268 T + ———
195 T + ———	232 F O ———	269 T + ———
196 T + ———	233 T + ———	270 T + ———
197 F O ———	234 F O ———	271 T + ———
198 T + ———	235 T + ———	272 F O ———
199 T + ———	236 T + ———	273 T + ———
200 T + ———	237 T + ———	274 F O ———
201 F O ———	238 T + ———	275 T + ———
202 F O ———	239 T + ———	276 T + ———
203 T + ———	240 F O ———	277 F O ———
204 F O ———	241 T + ———	278 T + ———
205 T + ———	242 T + ———	279 T + ———
206 T + ———	243 T + ———	280 T + ———
207 F O ———	244 T + ———	281 F O ———
208 T + ———	245 T + ———	282 T + ———
209 T + ———	246 T + ———	283 T + ———
210 F O ———	247 T + ———	284 T + ———
211 T + ———	248 T + ———	285 F O ———
212 T + ———	249 F O ———	
213 T + ———	250 T + ———	

Number of "correct" answers →
This is your total score.

Pain Test Score Sheet (Partial Score)

The "correct" answer in *all* items of the CW (contrasting words) scale is F or O.

Item Number	Your Answer Was	Check (√) If Correct
1	———	———
2	———	———
3	———	———
5	———	———
6	———	———
13	———	———
20	———	———
25	———	———
26	———	———
33	———	———
35	———	———
39	———	———
41	———	———
42	———	———
48	———	———
58	———	———
65	———	———
76	———	———
79	———	———
81	———	———
84	———	———
85	———	———
87	———	———
94	———	———
96	———	———
99	———	———
100	———	———
101	———	———
102	———	———
103	———	———
106	———	———
107	———	———
111	———	———
131	———	———
132	———	———
134	———	———
139	———	———
141	———	———

Pain Test Score Sheet (cont.)

Item Number	Your Answer Was	Check (✓) If Correct
142	——	——
146	——	——
149	——	——
150	——	——
154	——	——
155	——	——
158	——	——
175	——	——
177	——	——
180	——	——
181	——	——
183	——	——
185	——	——
188	——	——
190	——	——
192	——	——
194	——	——
197	——	——
201	——	——
202	——	——
204	——	——
207	——	——
210	——	——
218	——	——
219	——	——
227	——	——
229	——	——
232	——	——
234	——	——
240	——	——
249	——	——
260	——	——
272	——	——
274	——	——
277	——	——
281	——	——
285	——	——

Number of "correct" answers ➤ ▢
This is your score on the CW scale.

Mark your totals on the following two scales in order to interpret your general pain score. We should assume that the more intense your perceived or manifest pain, the more usefulness the discussion on pain has for you. Pain can be an asset to fulfillment in life.

Total Score

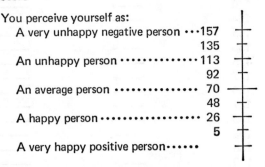

You perceive yourself as:
A very unhappy negative person ···157
135
An unhappy person ·············113
92
An average person ···············70
48
A happy person ···················26
5
A very happy positive person······

CW (contrasting words, or pleasure) Score

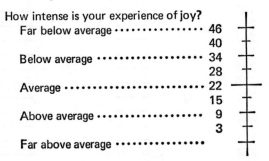

How intense is your experience of joy?
Far below average ·················46
40
Below average ····················34
28
Average ·························22
15
Above average ···················9
3
Far above average ················

Now proceed to develop your Pain Profile. Use the following worksheets to ascertain your partial scores. You will receive a score for each of eight types of pain or negative experiences—from frustration (F-scale) to meaninglessness (M-scale). Then plot your profile in the Pain Profile blank provided.

Pain Test Score Sheet (Partial Score)

The "correct" answer in *all* items of the F (frustration) scale is T or +.

Item Number	Your Answer Was	Check (✓) If Correct
8	——	——
9	——	——
17	——	——
18	——	——
29	——	——
30	——	——
36	——	——
50	——	——
51	——	——
54	——	——
61	——	——
63	——	——
68	——	——
78	——	——
82	——	——
89	——	——
97	——	——
98	——	——
105	——	——
110	——	——
112	——	——
113	——	——
114	——	——
117	——	——
125	——	——
126	——	——
145	——	——
151	——	——
157	——	——
159	——	——
162	——	——
187	——	——
193	——	——
198	——	——
200	——	——
203	——	——
217	——	——
226	——	——
258	——	——
262	——	——

Pain Test Score Sheet (cont.)

Item Number	Your Answer Was	Check (✓) If Correct
273	——	——
275	——	——
276	——	——

Total number of correct answers →
This is your score on the F scale.
Now plot it on your Pain Profile.

Pain Test Score Sheet (Partial Score)

The "correct" answer in *all* items of the P (physical pain) scale is T or +.

Item Number	Your Answer Was	Check (✓) If Correct
4	——	——
21	——	——
24	——	——
34	——	——
37	——	——
40	——	——
47	——	——
49	——	——
71	——	——
90	——	——
119	——	——
121	——	——
144	——	——
163	——	——
170	——	——
171	——	——
174	——	——
195	——	——
214	——	——
220	——	——
230	——	——
237	——	——
245	——	——
279	——	——

Total number of "correct" answers →
This is your score on the P scale.
Now plot it on your Pain Profile.

Pain Test Score Sheet (Partial Score)

The "correct" answer in *all* items of the A (anxiety and dread) scale is T or +.

Item Number	Your Answer Was	Check (√) If Correct
7	——	——
10	——	——
19	——	——
27	——	——
28	——	——
59	——	——
60	——	——
72	——	——
95	——	——
116	——	——
148	——	——
153	——	——
165	——	——
172	——	——
178	——	——
189	——	——
208	——	——
211	——	——
233	——	——
235	——	——
236	——	——
238	——	——
263	——	——
268	——	——

Total number of "correct" answers →

This is your score on the A scale.
Now plot it on your Pain Profile.

Pain Test Score Sheet (Partial Score)

The "correct" answer in *all* items of the L (loneliness) scale is T or +.

Item Number	Your Answer Was	Check (✓) If Correct
12	————	————
14	————	————
62	————	————
70	————	————
77	————	————
80	————	————
91	————	————
92	————	————
115	————	————
116	————	————
128	————	————
137	————	————
143	————	————
147	————	————
152	————	————
153	————	————
168	————	————
169	————	————
189	————	————
191	————	————
196	————	————
205	————	————
206	————	————
208	————	————
247	————	————
268	————	————
269	————	————

Total number of "correct" answers →

This is your score on the L scale.
Now plot it on your Pain Profile.

Pain Test Score Sheet (Partial Score)

The "correct" answer in *all* items of the T (tragedy and conflict) scale is T or +.

Item Number	Your Answer Was	Check (√) If Correct
15	———	———
16	———	———
43	———	———
44	———	———
46	———	———
52	———	———
93	———	———
173	———	———
199	———	———
221	———	———
223	———	———
233	———	———
235	———	———
238	———	———
241	———	———
242	———	———
243	———	———
250	———	———
253	———	———
265	———	———
280	———	———
283	———	———

Total number of "correct" answers →

This is your score on the T scale.
Now plot it on your Pain Profile.

Pain Test Score Sheet (Partial Score)

The "correct" answer in *all* items of the G (guilt) scale is T or +.

Item Number	Your Answer Was	Check (✓) If Correct
22	——	——
23	——	——
24	——	——
55	——	——
56	——	——
60	——	——
66	——	——
82	——	——
91	——	——
104	——	——
120	——	——
122	——	——
129	——	——
147	——	——
161	——	——
176	——	——
184	——	——
196	——	——
212	——	——
215	——	——
228	——	——
254	——	——
256	——	——
261	——	——
267	——	——
282	——	——
284	——	——

Total number of "correct" answers →

This is your score on the G scale.
Now plot it on your Pain Profile.

Pain Test Score Sheet (Partial Score)

The "correct" answer in *all* items of the D (depression) scale is T or +.

Item Number	*Your Answer Was*	*Check (✓) If Correct*
11	——	——
31	——	——
45	——	——
49	——	——
53	——	——
57	——	——
64	——	——
67	——	——
69	——	——
75	——	——
77	——	——
83	——	——
86	——	——
88	——	——
109	——	——
118	——	——
123	——	——
127	——	——
129	——	——
130	——	——
135	——	——
136	——	——
138	——	——
156	——	——
164	——	——
166	——	——
176	——	——
182	——	——
186	——	——
199	——	——
205	——	——
209	——	——
213	——	——
216	——	——
231	——	——
239	——	——
242	——	——
244	——	——
246	——	——
248	——	——

Pain Test Score Sheet (cont.)

	Your *Answer Was*	*Check ( )* *If "Correct"*
251	——	——
252	——	——
255	——	——
266	——	——
267	——	——
271	——	——
278	——	——
282	——	——

Total number of "correct" answers →
This is your score on the D scale.
Now plot it on your Pain Profile.

Pain Test Score Sheet (Partial Score)

The "correct" answer in *all* items of the M (meaninglessness) scale is **T or**

+.

Item Number	*Your Answer Was*	*Check (✓) If Correct*
11	———	———
32	———	———
38	———	———
53	———	———
67	———	———
69	———	———
73	———	———
74	———	———
80	———	———
108	———	———
115	———	———
116	———	———
124	———	———
130	———	———
133	———	———
135.	———	———
136	———	———
138	———	———
140	———	———
160	———	———
166	———	———
167	———	———
174	———	———
179	———	———
182	———	———
222	———	———
224	———	———
225	———	———
257	———	———
259	———	———
264	———	———
268	———	———
269	———	———
270	———	———
271	———	———

Total number of "correct" answers → ☐
This is your score on the M scale.
Now plot it on your Pain Profile.

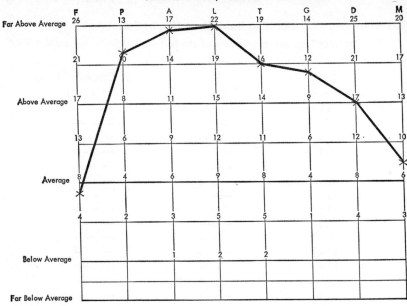

Figure 1

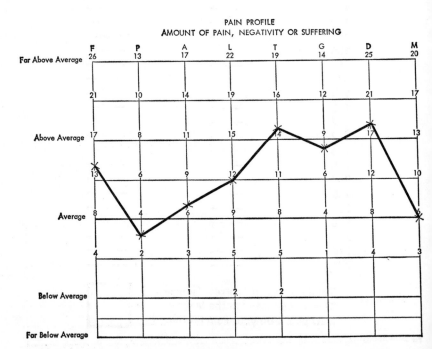

Figure 2

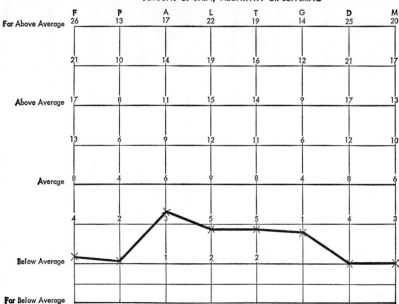

Figure 3

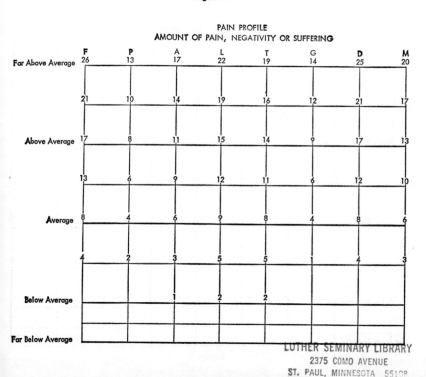

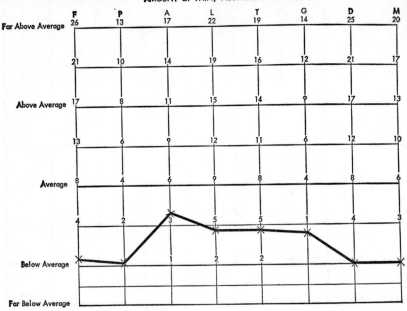

Figure 3

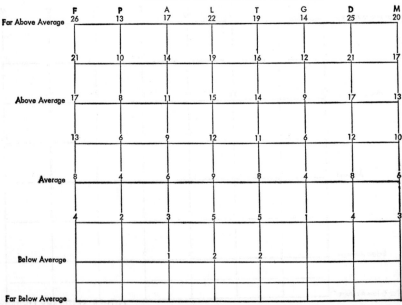

Your profile will suggest to you which areas of pain or negation are most intense in your life. Those sections dealing with your higher-intensity negative experiences or pains may then be the most useful ones for you. For example, Figure 1 represents an individual with somewhat high manifest pain in life. In fact, his total score is 107, which defines him as an unhappy person. His CW score is 15, which makes him a person of slightly above average manifest joy. The therapeutic strategy suggested by his profile is to focus on at least the exploration of anxiety and loneliness as the source of his meaning in life. The unique cognitive character of these two emotions is likely to be his most effective entry into philosophical depth and emotional authenticity. This person is not frustrated and seems to find his life quite meaningful. He does have a syndrome of physical pain, anxiety, loneliness (above all), conflict (T), guilt, and some depression. That sequence does in fact describe that person's being-in-the-world quite accurately.

Now look at Figure 2. Here we find less pain. Nevertheless, the cluster of manifest negation in this person's life is found in the areas of tragedy, guilt, and depression. These are the pains that are to be discussed and examined first. It is in these pains that the individual will be most helped by and responsive to philosophical insights about the meaning of his life. This person has practically no physical pain; his life seems quite meaningful to him. He has a low level of anxiety, but there is a little loneliness and some frustration in his life.

Finally, in Figure 3 we find a very happy person. Nevertheless, if we want to discuss his life philosophically, we are urged by his responses to focus on his experience of anxiety. This person has no physical pain, is not in the least depressed or frustrated. He is slightly lonely and has some conflict but no guilt, *just some anxiety*. That describes the meaning of negation in his life.

You the reader are invited to examine your own Profile.

10:

What Is Pain?

Ted

Ted is an unmarried thirty-one-year-old high school history teacher. He has a splendid grasp of the existential process which finds in the depths of despair the answer to life's psychological problems. He shows us the truth of the first great existential insight about pain: its cognitive character. Suffering and pain disclose to us regions deeply buried within, to which we have scant access without this maturing catharsis. Here is an eloquent record, taken from his journal, of the catharsis of Ted's feelings. He allows us to witness the transformation from depression to joy, from anxiety to peace, and from despair to hope. The statement is worth reading in its entirety. It will put us in touch with the experience of pain.

The ideas expressed in this Journal resulted from situations in which I was deeply involved in life. These experiences were filled with intense emotions of despair and joy as I climbed out of a darkened pit in which I felt helplessly lost and void of meaning to a point where I seemed to be one with God.

These personal encounters deal with problems that are of concern to Existentialism; the meaninglessness of existence, the purposelessness of man's life, man's struggle to find meaning while being caught up in nothingness, the threat of non-being, and finally, the discovery of man's ultimate freedom to confer value on his life. I have come to grips with these problems through intense encounters with life.

January 19

I am alone, desperately, painfully alone. Is there any purpose or meaning to my life? Is there an ultimate direction for me to discover? Why am I dissatisfied with my present existence, is there no way to still this passionate urge to be something more than what I am? My mind is disjointed, disorganized, I am losing contact with myself.

Nothing seems to hold meaning for me any more, at least not the kind of meaning that satisfies me. I realize that as a teacher I'm expendable, the school system can function without me, my students will miss me for a while, but I doubt that any child's life has been profoundly affected by my teaching or by my personality. My friends and loved ones can live without me. I want to have meaning for others, and it is only a supreme position of importance with which I will be satisfied and right now I am without importance.

At times I have perceived my seemingly infinite potential, I have caught glimpses of what it is to be God. It is this identification with God that I seek, this ultimate unity rests dormant within my soul and I feel compelled to give it life for it is the source of my meaning. Will I ever find this meaning which I so desperately seek? Oh God, the futility of my search, the impotency of my mortal mind, how can I find you, how can I be united with the infinite Thou?

The thought of my separateness, my absolute distinction eats away at me. I begin to feel threatened for I have always had faith in the existence of ultimate meaning and purpose. It has always seemed to me that my loneliness could be overcome, but I have never found the way. Now, more so than ever before I realize that I stand alone on this planet, God seems far off, even nonexistent.

I feel that I am forced into this position of loneliness and I rebel against having no choice in the matter. Yes, it's my freedom, my absolute independence that frightens me. I was placed here without having any say, and I was put here alone, and for what reason, what purpose do I have? I desperately want my meaning and purpose to be made clear to me. I want to understand, what is the niche I am destined to fill? Life would be so much easier if it were programmed, if meaning and purpose were built into me. Why can't I understand? Why did God leave it up to me to discover what I am? My freedom, my absolute independence terrifies me. I want to escape from my predicament but I can't, I'm trapped!

I have no meaning, God has left me alone, I am deathly afraid that without meaning I will be nothing. Tears of desperation flow down my cheeks. Violently I sob, meaning and purpose have been drained from me, I sink into total despair and absolute isolation, I am nothing! I realize finally and absolutely that no outside relationship can change the fact that I can only be alone, distinct and separate. No matter how I try to overcome my isolation, whether through means of loving God, man, woman or other, I am still alone. I must realize and accept this fact of my existence.

I now feel completely drained of emotion. The tears cease, I lay still as a wonderful calm sweeps over me. My thoughts have ceased for I am void of meaning and purpose, thought has no function, I have no function, no purpose, I am empty, I am nothing.

I feel relieved and somehow satisfied. A flash of insight illuminates my world. I begin to feel self confident, a new vitality wells up in my being. I realize that my mistake has been to seek meaning outside of my life. How has this obvious truth eluded me for so long! It's been right before my eyes. No, that is the very reason that the truth, my truth, has eluded me. I have relied on the information which my senses have brought to me, I've based my knowledge of reality only on what I could see, hear, taste and smell. Because I've neglected the *subject* of my experience, I've gone outside the source from which my perceptions emanate. Of course I'm empty of meaning, if I had meaning built into my life then I wouldn't be able to direct my own life, I would be determined by forces which I couldn't control, I would have no free choice. It is the very fact of my absolute aloneness that gives me the ultimate power and freedom that I seek. In my uniqueness and individuality rests the true value and meaning of my self, in this separateness I find my freedom.

I now begin to understand, to really understand the true meaning of my self. I understand that my absolute separateness is the reason for my freedom. I understand that outside approval and acceptance is not necessary for my survival.

Absurd visions begin to play in my mind, visions of a fool attempting to find his place in life by seeking the acceptance of others who have no idea where they are in life. I see a world of fools leading each other around in a blind attempt to hide from their true nature. I see fools pursuing meaningless goals which they believe will help them overcome the separateness they fear but the separateness and emptiness which in actuality is the very source of their freedom.

I laugh uproariously at the irony of the panorama that unfolds before me. The tears stream down my face, never before have I laughed so hard. What a tremendous feeling, what a tremendous relief. I feel purged and gloriously free. I think not of my separateness, but of my freedom. This realization of the real meaning of my isolation has freed me of the categories in which others have placed me, and in which I have placed myself. I am freed of the bonds of status and prestige. I am no longer threatened, for what I was threatened by before doesn't exist. I realize now that I am the source of my own value, I can not gain value and direction from factors outside myself in the way I once perceived.

My true self is coming to fruition. I am discovering myself by realizing what I am not. I am not a teacher, a son, a lover, a philosopher, not even a man. In a way I am all these people, but I am also much more, infinitely more, and I must not limit my essence to the idea of these illusions. I can lose my job, my house, my lover, and I will still be here.

I laugh at my self for what I have often thought of my self as being. I laugh at the absurdity of seeking identity through the possession of status and material possessions. The freedom that I have always sought is right here! What a wonderful thought, I seek my self and here I am.

I must not hold on so tightly to the things I once thought were responsible for giving meaning and value to my life. My job, possessions, friends, lovers and even my ideas have been grasped so tightly that my life has been strangled. Relaxation is so important! By releasing my grip on life I allow true experience to filter through.

I feel close to God. The loneliness I felt before was caused by the fact that I was seeking identity and security by trying to possess things and ideas which I believed were essential aspects of my self but in reality were far removed from the consciousness which I realize my self to be. My loneliness was an extreme reaction against trying to unite with things foreign to my nature.

Again I am filled with emotion, only these tears that burst forth are tears of joy. I fall on my knees, throw up my arms to heaven and cry out my thanks to God for my freedom. I delight in the pure joy of mere being. At last I am at peace with my self and with the idea that God is the supreme conscious awareness that I am.

January 20

What an exhilarating experience to be totally involved in life. Whenever I encounter the basic problems of life head-on, regardless of the emotions I feel at the time, I always come out of the experience feeling charged with energy, self-confident and with a positive attitude toward life.

My involvement with the eternal present has enabled me to contact the real meaning of my existence. I realize the importance of concentrating on the present moment. A diffused mind that is filled with value judgments and presuppositions wanders to and fro from past to future missing reality completely.

Ted, with his profound and tearful experience, can teach us a universe about the management of pain.

Dr. Louis Shattuck Baer, a professor of internal medicine at the Stanford Medical School, sends his patients more often to the library than to the pharmacy. The *Palo Alto Times* reports his views as follows:[1]

1 *Palo Alto Times,* Oct. 5, 1971. Reprinted by permission.

DOCTOR FINDS PHILOSOPHY WORKS BETTER THAN MEDICINE

"Almost 30 years as a family physician have taught me that the precepts of philosophy surpass medicine or surgery as therapy for many of my patients," he says.

One of Dr. Baer's unusual theories is that suffering is necessary to man's existence.

"It's my belief that suffering is as necessary as oxygen, nitrogen or carbon for man's origins, his evolution and his continued existence," he says. "If this is understood, then perhaps we can seek to mitigate it with better proportions of calculative and meditative thinking than is seen in the practice of medicine today.

"Where philosophy becomes important is in treating the patient who has a chronic illness he must live with or an illness which will be fatal.

"It's also valuable in dealing with the patient who's worried to the extent that it's making him sick, and the patient who's run out of hope, who sees his case as hopeless."

Dr. Baer feels "there frequently is not enough time in the regular medical program for a consideration of the philosophic implications in both diagnosis and treatment."

It is the responsibility of a compassionate philosophy to use whatever knowledge it has acquired toward the amelioration of suffering. Kindness is still man's great value.

Pain is a three-dimensional phenomenon; it has an x, y, and z axis. It has height, width, and depth. Let us begin with an analysis of the heights to which pain can rise.

The Height of Pain

Pain runs the gamut from the inevitable, such as old age and death, on the one end, to the avoidable, such as injustice and tooth decay, on the other. For each of these categories philosophy has a different response.

Pain that is avoidable today, such as paralysis from polio, was a threat to all children just a few years ago. There is thus a category of totally unnecessary pain.

There is also the category of pain, such as cancer, against which the rational man struggles by enlisting all his will and intelligence. Philosophy can help here by giving man the *will* to fight and by showing him that in this struggle he can find his destiny and the meaning of his life.

Finally, there is the pain that is truly and forever inevitable. It is the pain suffered by the most successful and the happiest of men. That is the pain of human finitude, which means death and frustration. It is also the pain of human freedom, which means anguish and guilt.

An existential philosophy addresses itself to this category of pain by pointing out what at first reading may appear paradoxical, even outrageous—namely, that *we choose our limitations freely because we know that they create the best possible life and the supreme happiness for us.* To understand this point is to have found the secret of personal maturity and human authenticity.

In the metaphysics of religion, this insight is translated into the statement "God, who is infinite, chooses to be human, which means finitude. In order to create himself as a human being, God must limit irrevocably his infinity. God chooses himself to be human because he knows that it is better to be human and finite than infinite and divine." The myth of creation is the story of that insight.

Philosophy can help each individual to recover that choice in the structure of his own consciousness. Existentially oriented therapy will help each person discover that he makes (and wants to make) that choice. This choice is at the root of all *unavoidable* individual human suffering. (Of particular interest here is the example of Waldo at the end of the next chapter.)

Exercise

This map of the "height" dimension of pain means little unless integrated into your daily existence. I suggest therefore the following exercise: make a short list of your problems. Then divide them into three groups: those that you can readily avoid, those against which you must struggle and might win, and those which you, like all human beings, must accept. In constructing your list remember that all three groups often overlap in what at first, before philosophical analysis, we call a single pain problem. Once your list is reasonably accurate and complete, develop a response and make a plan on how to deal with your pain.

Following is an example of Pain Exercise I, taken from the journal of Roland, a thirty-two-year-old electrical engineer, married, with two children.

A blank is included for your own use.

Name: <u>Roland B.</u>

Pain Exercise I. The Spectrum of Pain.

A. List several troublesome pains in your life.
   1. Too many colds.
   2. Constant car trouble.
   3. Hate the smog.
   4. Job is good but not meaning-giving.
   5. Getting older without adequate achievement.
   6. I have conflicts about mother, who should
      be placed in some kind of a home. I worry
      about the money and I am afraid she will
      move in with us.
   7. I am an outward success but inside me I am
      depressed and confused.
   8. I am afraid of being mugged.

B. Analysis. Reorganize the above pains into the
   following three groups (keep in mind that each
   pain is composite), explain your thinking and
   offer solutions.
   1. Pains that I can easily avoid:
      Colds and car trouble can be helped with
   better planning and more intelligent living
   (regular hours, healthier foods). I can
   afford a better car and I think I will buy
   one. I have been too lazy.
      Mugging. I can avoid dangerous times and
   places, even though I would be restricted. I
   can get better locks for the house.

   2. Pains against which I can struggle:
      Smog. I can try to earn more and move out
   of the area. I can look for a job where the
   air is clean. I can try to persuade my wife,
   who likes it here, to move.
      I can use my skills to help fight air pollu-
   tion. In fact, I have wanted for some time
   now to join an activist group in the war against

pollution. If I make a commitment for social involvement some of my guilt will be dissipated. Such work will give me meaning.

Job. I can look for ways to improve my job. In fact, some of us at the laboratory are getting together on a regular basis to see how we can humanize our jobs more. I could be really courageous and look for a second career that may give me greater meaning. I think I would like to go into medicine. On second thought, I think I'll make a proposal to Dr. G., the lab general manager, about practical ways to humanize the job. I have some constructive ideas. In fact, I'll write them up and submit it as an article for publication in one of the trade journals.

3. Pains that I cannot avoid:
Mother's oncoming death.

My inner sense of depression about the meaningless of life.

My anxiety of getting old without achieving anything.

I think I need philosophy to deal with these problems.

Diagnosis

On the basis of the avoidable-unavoidable classification of pain (what is called here the ladder or the height dimension), we can offer Roland the following simplified diagnosis.

The pains listed under B 1 require for their amelioration little more than willpower and determination. Willpower results from understanding and exercising the freedom with which all of us are born. Roland must be helped to experientially rediscover the freedom that defines his human nature. He can then use this knowledge to bring about the minor modifications listed under B 1.

The pains listed under B 2 may never be removed, although there is hope. Roland must resolve to fight. His answer is to be found in his protest. Roland is alienated, and the struggle against his depression is his answer because it becomes his connection with the world. Also, the struggle is his meaning; it gives him something important and something real to do. The struggle against pollution and against the dehumanization occuring on the job in the corporation will help him recognize his worth: others need him. Finally, the humane causes will give him commitment; through them, he will express his responsibility to his fellow man. He will cease being an isolated individual and become a social being. Roland needs that challenge for the creation of his meaning. He will find that, far from being threatened by redirecting his profession and his education, he will instead redirect his life from depression to joy.

But in order to deal with the pains that he lists under B 3—separation from mother, death, anxiety, and the general meaninglessness of existence—Roland needs philosophy. He has to learn to recognize that *being* Roland means being separated from his mother, facing ceaselessly the responsibility of creating his own meanings, and being eventually separated from life by death.

But he also must make the philosophic discovery that *he wants to be Roland* or at least that *he has chosen to be Roland.* If he now rechooses himself as Roland or rededicates himself to the choice already made, he will have achieved existential authenticity. Rephrasing Tertullian's famous *credo ut intelligam,* one must first *make* the choice in order then to realize that he *wants* to make it.

John, a thirty-five-year-old policeman who is in the process of making important personal and professional changes in his life, has an entry in his journal that I quote below. He describes well the agony involved in choosing to be himself.

> Several days ago I experienced myself and my world in a way which is difficult to describe. My day was very rich. Not that it was pure pleasure or a day of rainbows. I had a major choice to make regarding a relationship which was painful for me. I had numerous experiences of my day but the most profound awareness was *my* awareness of the movement of my existence through each moment or event. I had a sense of homecoming or centeredness. That each event, each moment was ME. I could feel that each awareness (depression, elation, intellectualism, lying on the grass, anxiety) I had was mine and I owned them. It seemed as if it was *MY* world and my inwardness flowed from moment to moment. I felt truly alive. I experienced my aliveness and being as being projected out into the world. I was the locus of me or my projections. It was my world and I felt Godlike. I didn't feel I was God but rather that I was not the trees and windmill being blown by the wind but that *I was the wind.* The unbounded feeling of movement was very exciting. While sitting in class, studying in the library, driving to school, making a choice to

leave a relationship, lying on the grass—all of these awareness were ME. I was the center of these experiences, I owned them.

Then something happened the next day. I awoke feeling a loss of me. I felt a profound sense of estrangement from myself. I was now being blown by the wind. My response was dread and anxiety in losing myself. I tried to recapture the day before— to reclaim me—to return to the center of myself and my world which I owned the day before. During my session with my therapist I screamed in horror at the loss of the sense of "being" and aliveness. As the painful session continued I started to experience that my pain, dread and estrangement was ME. What I was the day before was then and me. And, what I was in that session was NOW and also me. As I began to experience ownership of my dread and loss of my "being" I had a sense of returning home, of centeredness, and of movement.

Looking back now, I feel that I experienced the "miracle of being" and the horror of non-being, or non-aliveness and death. Perhaps the profound impact, awe and bewilderment of being alive and a sense of having touched God put me in touch with my resistance of the death of myself as a totally alive human being.

11:

The Depth of Pain

Every pain comes in layers. And each successive layer that is exposed in stripping pain down to its core gives us additional philosophical information about our nature as human beings. Pain is cognitive: it leads to philosophic knowledge about the meaning of being a person. The exploration of the layers of pain—the "mining" of pain—is central to self-disclosure (theme B of the Master Table). If in mining pain we discover our individual nature, we are involved in psychotherapy, whereas if the gold we find is true of all men, we are dealing in essences and thus involved in philosophy. A tragic sense of life is prerequisite to understanding ourselves. We must prize this opportunity for self-knowledge, because it is only through pain that the essence of our humanity, our differences from the animals and from the gods, can be fully understood and appreciated. (These insights are consolidated in themes C 1, C 2, and C 14 of the Master Table.) Our happiness-oriented culture is an escape from the responsibility of understanding ourselves.

In the existential personality theory the surface layer of our pains is called neurotic, pathological, or inauthentic pain. That is the pain which concerns physicians, surgeons, and therapists. It is the pain which results from illness and can be "cured" with drugs, surgery, and therapy. It is pain which destroys the body and paralyzes the mind, truncates meaningful human relationships and limits effective interaction with the environment. Within this chapter we will distinguish briefly between deep, medium, and surface layers of suffering by using the example of guilt. At this point you might find it useful to refer to the earlier discussion of guilt which opens Chapter 6.

Deep layers of pain disclose what existential philosophers call *ontological* pain. That pain is philosophical, authentic, and existential. It is typically human, "incurable"; it is strength-giving and inspiring. The deepest, ontological, layers of pain define the meaning of human existence.

The upper layers, the *surface* levels of pain—neurotic pains—are frequently "second-order" pains. They are pains about pains. Examples would be anxiety about anxiety, guilt about guilt, and the resentment of injustice.

The meaning of the concept of layers of guilt can be clarified through an illustration. Gloria, a legal secretary, married for eleven years and childless, is tempted into an affair with one of her boss's clients. She feels guilty; in fact, she faces several layers of guilt. Her deepest level of guilt is ontological, for it is the conflict between un-fulfiled possibilities (if she rejects the affair) and violation of a trust-ing relationship (her husband loves and trusts her). This conflict—either choice leads to guilt—is ontological because it exists in the very nature of human beings and the social world into which we are born. She can be helped to gain strength and comfort from the insight that her deepest layer of guilt is as much part of her humanity as is the circulation of her blood and her breathing.

A *medium* layer of guilt is learned. It is a social, tribal, or anthro-pological phenomenon rather than an ontological or philosophical one. Society has taught Gloria the powerful force of two conflicting claims: (1) love is good and must be sought and (2) adultery is a sin and must be avoided. Whichever way Gloria chooses—husband or affair—she will have violated a social canon and will thus feel guilt. That is the guilt of her superego, her conscience; it is the guilt arising from a violation of the internalized rule, the rule introjected by a foreign authority. This medium or social level of conflict is not to be confused with the deep or philosophical level discussed above. Medium, or social guilt can be allayed only through a change in culture. Deep or philosophical guilt is embedded in the eternal nature of human exist-ence.

Gloria experiences guilt while she believes "normal" and "healthy" people do not suffer from guilt or guilt feelings. She feels guilty, in the sense of feeling both inadequate and responsible for that inadequacy. Surface guilt comes from violating the demands of conformism. Gloria's surface guilt is her feeling that she "is different" or is not "keeping up with her friends." Surface guilt may also be the fear that she does not conform to her parents' wishes.

There are then at least three layers of guilt: philosophical, social, and psychological. Only the last two are subject to change: social guilt through cultural transformations and psychological guilt through psychotherapy. Philosophical guilt can only be understood and ac-cepted; it cannot be changed. Whereas social and psychological guilt are damaging—they truncate the growth of the individual and must be overcome through therapy and social action—philosophical guilt can be illuminating, self-disclosing, and invigorating. Philosophical guilt puts man in touch with his essence and thereby gives him the strength to choose himself, to embrace himself and his destiny and thus live fully.

How can philosophy help Gloria understand and manage her dilemma? Philosophy can show her that the surface layers of guilt are based on ignorance. When philosophical wisdom is integrated into her life she can be free of needless pain, thus making room for a constructive use of ontological pain. Surface pain hides the truth and debilitates the spirit, whereas the depth of pain is the challenge that makes life real and meaningful. Her unavoidable and thus real guilt is the conflict between two values: loyalty (to her husband) and love (in the affair). Conflict itself is an ultimate philosophic reality about man (theme C 14 of the Master Table), because each of these incompatible values separately is an essential truth about human existence. When Gloria recognized that her guilt was the full depth of her human situation, she gained strength and inspiration from the challenge, rather than the ineffectiveness that had previously been expressed by her anxiety about that guilt. She overcame the suspicion that she was inferior and had a problem that she could not resolve. In fact, meeting this challenge—more than choosing between being loyal or being loving—was what eventually gave joy and meaning to her life. After one year of confronting the challenge of her existential conflict, Gloria left her husband *and* the affair. She ultimately entered into a new marriage on a far more mature basis than anything she had ever done up to that point in her life.

Exercise

Let us continue with the effort to inject these insights into your living situations. We again use Roland's journal. Roland is asked to analyze his pains and determine what portion of them is ontological (and thus responsive to philosophic "treatment") and what part is not, and thus is based on philosophic ignorance and lack of self-disclosure. Use Roland's answers as guidelines to develop your own answers for Pain Exercise II. Use the blank provided.

How can deep ontological or philosophical pain be integrated into life? How can life be better because of pain based on the philosophical nature of man?

Name: <u>Roland B.</u>

Pain Exercise II.   The Layers of Pain.

A. Describe what you believe to be the ontological, authentic, existential or philosophic layer of the pains that you examined in Exercise I.   List at least two elements of that layer.

My life has no meaning because life in general has no meaning.   I can and must give and assign meanings to my life.   I see that and it is clear to me that I have the free will to do it.

B. What do you propose to do to manage the pain on a philosophical level?

I must and can decide what really is important to me in life.   I must have the courage to realize that I have pursued false gods for most of three decades.   I become strong as I permit myself to feel the grief of stupidly having thrown away life's most precious values for so many years.   I hurt, but the hurt makes me strong—as long as I can feel it.   It is an almost physical sensation in my chest.   I can imagine how superstitious people believe God or a Spirit has entered them and given them strength, or eternal life, or something like that.

Right now I feel free and have no difficulty in determining my real values.   I want to love my wife and be loved by her.   I want to love my two children and be loved by them.   I want to be a good father to my Melissa and Kathy so they can be proud of me when they are grown women.

I also want to contribute to society through my electrical engineering profession.   I genuinely want to improve the world and be appreciated for being of service.   I guess I yearn for warm relationships with people rather than aloof connections with mathematical abstractions and with tapes and computers, lathes and solder.

I will be more affectionate with my family and more dedicated on my job. I will be more help-ful and thoughtful towards the men who work for me.

Pain Exercise II. The Layers of Pain.

A. Describe what you believe to be the ontological, authentic, existential or philosophic layer of the pains that you examined in Exercise I. List at least two elements of that layer.

_____

_____

_____

_____

B. What do you propose to do to manage the pain on a philosophical level?

_____

_____

_____

_____

_____

_____

_____

_____

_____

_____

_____

_____

_____

_____

_____

_____

_____

_____

_____

The Meaning of Negation

Negation is the essence of pain. What does that mean? [1] Take any experience of pain whatever—moral, physical, or emotional—and reduce it to its general and final meaning. You will find that in any and all pain the individual ego discovers that the world says "no" to him; pain is the "no" of the world. Pain, as negation, is the experience of the boundaries that the world imposes on man. The problem of pain thus becomes the problem of managing man's finitude. And this is an important conclusion.

You can now rephrase for yourself the problem of pain. Your life is surrounded by walls, barriers, boundaries, absolute limits. How do you feel about the idea of limits in general? Do you feel like a prisoner who is held back, who is deprived of the real and the desirable world beyond? Or do you instead feel like an animal in a zoo, protected in your cage from the threats of the onrushing and unpredictable crowds? Are these boundaries like moats which keep you from climbing into the castle? Or are they instead more like mountains which you love to climb? Your answer to these questions is critical. If the idea of a limit is a prison, then the world is essentially evil. If, however, the idea of a limit represents to you a zone of protection or is for you an invigorating challenge, like climbing a mountain to achieve a spectacular view, then it is precisely these limits that give both reality and meaning to your life.

Let us assume your answer is the former and that your limits in life are so severe as to embitter you. Ask yourself if you can move your limits back far enough to change them from being frustrating to being challenging. We can symbolize this transformation by thinking of a heavy castle gate which imprisons you. By pushing on the gate, you can make it lean over to cover the moat and act as a bridge. What at first frustrated you now has been changed sufficiently—without being destroyed—to aid you in your movement toward freedom.

Ultimately, it is finitude that is intolerable. The man who affirms the glory of his existence by saying "yes" to life must learn to manage

1 Rather than "pain" or "suffering," we should use the philosophical term "negation" to refer to painful experiences generally. The philosophy of religion has called our question the problem of evil. The Book of Job in the *Old Testament* is devoted to this problem, called theodicy. The Bible asks, in effect, What does evil mean in the perspective of a world dominated by an infinitely good and all-powerful God? Our philosophic question therefore becomes, "What is the meaning of negation? What does negation, the negative in life, tell us about the values of life? How can philosophy help us come to terms with the negative in life? How can we ever truthfully say that we choose negation from the infinite freedom of our inward consciousness?"

this unacceptable condition. The first step in the management of negation is to recognize that pain is real. Our society conspires against that
knowledge. We live in a pill-pushing and pill-popping society. A pill
can dull the senses and stupefy the mind, but it cannot help human
beings come to terms with the ineluctable realities of negation. A pill
hides the truth and makes the task of attaining philosophic insight
just that much more arduous.

The discovery of negation is the discovery of our human essence.
Each pain, each negation, uncovers its own unique human essence.
Negation, in disclosing our human essence, shows to us the phenomena
of (1) *constitution* (A 3 on the Master Table), (2) The *Other* (C 9 and
C 10 on the Master Table), and (3) *the desirability of finitude* (C 1, C 2,
and C 14). In a larger sense, the existence of negation makes possible
such human desiderata as growth (C 13) and life itself (C 8).

Constitution and the Other

Constitution means that I, as a free and responsible agent, create, organize, produce, or bring about a particular way of perceiving reality.
Specifically, constitution of the *Other* means that I assume responsibility for creating a world for myself in which an independent Other
is the central feature. Constitution of *finitude* means that I assume
full, deliberate, free, and creative responsibility for my own limits,
my own finitude. In short, I choose myself as finite. If I were God, I
would, in my infinite wisdom, relinquish my infinity and voluntarily
limit myself as a human being. That is the meaning of the constitution of finitude. Thus, constitution requires negation, the existence
of the Other implies negation, and the choice of finitude is an act of
negation. Therefore, all the phenomena that are the essence of consciousness—constitution, the Other, and finitude—contain the element
of pain in their being.

For anything to exist and to be known, its opposite is required. The
Latin word *existere* means, literally, "to stand out"; to exist is for
something to come into being and then to call attention to itself by
being different from its background. Contrast is needed for existence,
experience, and perception. Light is not something perceived in itself:
it is manifested to the experiencing organism only after it has met its
"other" and has been reflected by it. Neither the concept nor the experience of light or day can exist except as they are brought into
relief through a background of shadow and night. If night did not
exist, we would have to invent it and preserve it in our imagination
to give meaning to the concept of daylight. In the process of creating,
constructing, or "constituting" the meaning of light, we automatically
and inevitably bring about the idea of night, its Other. As with the

magnet used to illustrate the concept of consciousness, or with electrical phenomena, a positive charge brings about (i.e., constitutes) its opposite, a negative charge. The negative charge is its Other, and the existence of the positive charge has no meaning and no reality without the existence of its Other.

Is that situation bad? Not at all. If we love music we do not denigrate silences because they momentarily rob us of sound. Every listener recalls the effective pause in the Halleluja Chorus of Handel's *Messiah*, in which the climactic notes are introduced by a conspicuous period of silence.

Furthermore, life is a meaningful concept only because of the idea of death. Again in this case we would have to invent our death in order to be aware of the fact that we are alive. Ask yourself, in full honesty, this question: If there were no death, real or imagined, would the statement "I am alive" have any meaning whatever? If life itself is man's greatest value, would he not have to invent death to be conscious of life?

This insight, that opposites create, is compressed in the very meaning of the word "definition" itself. To define means to delimit, to set boundaries, because to bring out the meaning of a concept is to show its borders, to indicate what it is *not*.

In a similar vein we can say that joy exists as a meaningful idea only because there also is suffering. The joy-suffering contrast is experienced vividly upon recovering from an illness. It is also found in the vertigo that follows hyperventilation. When the patient experiences some relief from the agonies of vertigo he slips into brief moments of euphoria. So much for constitution.

Let us now move from our specific analysis of constitution to a consideration of the Other. The only answer to loneliness and aloneness is the discovery that there exists another—person, animal, or natural object—in this world. The Other is our roots. In our society, which pays lip service to mobility and independence, not enough attention is given to the feelings of rootedness and the need for a home. Even enemies are preferable to no one at all, a fact seen in the relationships that sometimes develop between prisoner and guard or criminal and victim. The Other is a necessary aspect of consciousness. The Other, by its nature, *opposes* the subject of consciousness. Sometimes this opposition is called hate, sometimes love. But always it is the Other. The Other can be a person or nature. Every experience in which we feel *real*, substantial, joyous, and alive is an experience in which we have discovered the reality of the Other; we have discovered that we are not alone in this world. Nature is real, not an illusion. People are real, not illusory. The world is real, and not a dream. If we were truly alone, like God before Creation, we indeed would have to invent the Other in order to feel real, to understand that we exist and to overcome our loneliness. Here we see the deep meaning of the myth of Creation: God creates Nature as His Other; thus the second root of pain lies in its Otherness. And Otherness is beautiful.

The Desirability of Finitude

We want negation; we choose it and assume full responsibility for it; negation is an aspect of man's supreme good.

It is cruel and insensitive, in fact even false, to tell someone who suffers deeply that he really *wants* his suffering and that his pain is really for the best. This is reminiscent of an older age in which pain, like poverty, was believed to be the result of moral depravity. The value I speak of here is different, and can best be illustrated with an example.

Waldo is an extremely talented twenty-three-year-old violinist. He has positions in several leading orchestras in the Western U.S., practices a major part of the time, and has been able to make unusual coaching arrangements with a couple of world-famous musicians. Recently, Waldo was offered a contract to play both the Beethoven and the Tchaikovski violin concerti in several solo performances with a top East Coast orchestra. Taping sessions for a major record company were also included in the contract. It was the opportunity of his lifetime. He commuted to rehearsals, which meant weekly flights across the United States. The first rehearsals were unexpectedly successful. Waldo had never played better in his life. The weekly flights were no problem, because he had flown from earliest childhood and even had a pilot's license. Although Waldo's family was from San Francisco, he had spent many years in Paris and also went to school in Rome, making frequent transatlantic flights. It came therefore as a disturbing surprise to Waldo that from the time of the signing of his contract as soloist he began to develop serious bouts of airsickness. As soon as he entered the airplane he would panic—as if he had suddenly developed claustrophobia. Once in the air, he became dizzy, nauseous, and blacked out for short periods of time. Flying, which all his life had been easy and fun for Waldo, now, at the height of his career and when he most depended on it, became an intolerable ordeal.

Following, in Waldo's own journal, is his record of how he attempted to deal philosophically with this catastrophic development.

September 3

I feel like total hell. I've never played better. I've never had a better opportunity to make it big. I am about to enter the big-league concert and recording career. I am on the threshold to greatness and I am too weak to take it! I feel fine and buoyant but I'm so sick on the plane that I would rather die than go on.

God dammit! I am going to decide to cope with this situation! "I choose to cope! I choose to cope!" That's what Dr. Koestenbaum used to say.[2] This choice is rational only; it is abstract. In truth, I don't want to cope. I've lost heart. But I do make the choice not to cope, to black out. I make it feebly. I will follow the instructions for this journal.

I am sick when I am most successful. I am myself stopping myself at the height of my career. I am suffering from what Dr. Koestenbaum calls the "hubris-nemesis syndrome." My consciousness is introducing negation into itself.

I get sick when I am up high. The height of the airplane is like the apex of my career, my playing. I stop myself at that height. My consciousness negates itself automatically. It is the collective unconscious, the ancient myth of man who is being punished for the arrogance of his success.

I can sense how self-negation is built into the structure of consciousness itself. "Each action produces an equal reaction." The more successful my consciousness is the more it puts on the brakes. Negation seems to resurface in myths, religion, philosophy, dreams and in the functioning of my body and psyche. Consciousness is like God, it cannot exist without its Other. My consciousness is soaring dangerously high, to God. It will lose itself if it continues to soar! My consciousness introduces the limits of its Otherness as if this were some ancient and deep wisdom.

I feel at this moment of my thinking that I am assuming responsibility for my airsickness! I feel euphoric. I seem at this very moment to be integrating my airsickness into my total life and a weight is lifted! But I fear that even this success is hubris and will not be permitted. It does give me a headache! I am condemned to fail even in the understanding of my failure. O God, I punish myself for my success and then I punish myself all over again for *understanding* that I punish myself for my success!

My airsickness is the Otherness that is thrown as limit into the face of my soaring ego, my flying consciousness. But it is true that my airsickness, if perceived in its philosophic truth, gives me a sense of being a concrete ego. I feel like a real self and a strong consciousness. For God's sake, let me admit once and for all that *I want to feel like hell! It is good for me to feel like hell! I want to place obstacles in the way of my violin! I love those obstacles! Those brakes are good!* My neck bulges and I feel like screaming!

Waldo has assumed free and full personal responsibility for the negation that exists so disturbingly in his life. He says he places it there, and he does so because he wants to. He knows that it is the mature functioning of consciousness that is involved. He knows that he is in touch with the structure of his pure consciousness, with the intentionality of being. His life is perceived by him to be an expression of the phenomenon of constitution itself. He senses with powerful directness how his consciousness is constituting Otherness and finitude in his life. And if he has any philosophic understanding at all, he would never have it otherwise.

His next step is to translate his philosophical discovery—that airsickness is his way of limiting the infinity of his consciousness for the sake of feeling *real*—more humanistically into his present life situation. The philosophical insight has appeared to him in an "impractical" way. The insight does what it says. It says, "You need negation" and it *gives* him that negation by making his life difficult. The insight itself is thus an instance of further negation. The insight in turn becomes the challenge. It is instructive to follow Waldo's journal—next is an entry written two months later—and his attempt to integrate the pain into a more mature life and better musicianship for him. His words express how suffering translates itself into meaning, pain into joy whenever we are in touch with the philosophic roots of negation.

November 10

I have discovered two ways of philosophically integrating my airsickness with my commitment to the violin. I have learned how to fight fate with my music; but I have also learned how to flow, in complete passivity, with life. As a result my playing has developed a virtuosity it did not have before. The conductor, Maestro G————, told me my playing had become sweet and mellow without losing the brilliance for which I had been known. He told me I played like a much older and more experienced musician than I was. Mr. D————, of the ————— ————— newspaper, told me the "authority" of my playing was that of a master. I now possessed maturity in addition to technical virtuosity.

My playing is not just an attack on frustration or obstacles. My fight is steep, like a parabolic curve. The more I fight the tougher the fight gets. I am always just a bit ahead of myself. Man, am I moving fast!

I let myself go with the stream of the conflict between the violin and the airsickness. I no longer try to fight *against* airsickness or *for* the violin.[3] I look at this conflict before me in my life, so intimate and threatening earlier, like a Shakespearean tragedy. I almost enjoy watching the ridiculous struggle between my soaring success, which recall the high notes on the E-string, and my nonsensical obstacle, like a string which nightmarishly breaks again and again. I feel I float weightless and silent on a

3 C 14 of the Master Table.

wave. The gates of my unconscious must be open and the contents freely released. My playing is easy. My nausea does not worry me. I laugh at it. It has changed my playing. I am no longer recognized as the same violinist. I move with the stream of the conflict the way a seagull floats on the waves of the ocean or a trout facing upstream is suspended completely still against the clear waters of a rushing stream. I have never felt this much at ease in my life before.

There is another thing. I play that conflict in my concerts. I rebel against it; I love it; I observe it; I overlook it. If you ask today, "What do you say with your playing?" my answer is "I celebrate the reality of consciousness by choosing its opposition. I give affect and lots of feeling to an abstract philosophical truth!"

The history of consciousness has once more reaffirmed itself, and this time in the life of Waldo. By choosing to cope, he has been able to assume responsibility for his pain and to experience it in that aspect which is truly self-willed. The self-willed aspect of pain appeared to him the moment he recognized the universal philosophical ingredient underlying his rather particularized problem.

A recording of one of Waldo's performances is among my most cherished possessions.

Remember

1. The only pain that concerns philosophy is the pain that is inevitable.

2. Try choosing to be what or who you already are. Try really to accept yourself for what you are. You will feel tremendous relief.

3. Your pains and frustrations will give depth and meaning to your life, if you can only learn how to *protest* vigorously against them.[4]

4. A tragic sense of life is the beginning of self-knowledge.

5. Negation in your life simply means you know you are real.

6. Negation in your life means you know you are never alone.

7. Negation in your life means you have put on your brakes to slow down in order to enjoy your trip.

[4] Protest, through the mechanism of no-saying, makes us conscious of the Other. As a result we experience the reality of our concrete individual existence.

12:

The Types of Pain

Although there is overlap, different kinds of pain disclose different aspects of human reality. Understanding what each individual pain can reveal to us about the philosophical essence of man is helpful in guiding each of us to the necessary existential phenomenological management of pain. For example, a person who suffers deeply from guilt would need to approach his program for philosophical self-disclosure differently from one whose principal problem was frustration. Whereas guilt may reveal the eternal freedom of man, frustration may reveal the ineluctable as well as desirable reality of the Other. Reference to your individual profile derived from the pain test (Chapter 9) is useful here.

The following are guidelines only, since a particular negative word does not always designate the same painful experience and even the same experience does not always yield predictable material.

Anxiety and Dread

Anxiety and dread represent some of the most important negative philosophical experiences. The exploration of the cognitive meaning of these experiences has long been associated with the foundation stone of existentialism itself. In other words, existentialism has long held that anxiety (*Angst,* anguish) reveals deep truths to us, truths not available through other means, such as the senses or scientific measurements. Furthermore, the truths thus revealed answer the questions associated with our needs for meaning, authenticity, and human fulfillment.

This cluster of negative experiences called anxiety and dread can be evoked by such words as *desperate* (or being in a state of despair or of sorrow), *agitated, afraid, awful, terrified, panicky, shaky, separated, lost, rejected, homeless,* and *unloved.*

Anxiety and dread are central to existential philosophy because they *disclose the transcendental dimension*—the region of pure consciousness in human experience, the reflective and reflexive (i.e., self-referential) observer of all events. The transcendental dimension is the pure zone of subjectivity, the observer who himself is never observed, the silent solitary center. In short, anxiety and dread disclose the nature of consciousness. And that is quite a discovery! Consciousness has been denied, ignored, and explained away. Anxiety reestablishes the reality of consciousness; it provides an experience which gives us direct access to the most important and the most central phenomenon of human existence: consciousness. Philosophically understood, then, anxiety is no longer a disease which embarrasses us and which must therefore be tranquillized.

Consciousness can also be understood intellectually; that was achieved by the philosopher René Descartes when he invented and applied the method of systematic and universal doubt. He accepted nothing that could be doubted. And because everything is subject to doubt, he would have become a skeptic except for one basic fact: the existence itself of consciousness cannot be doubted. It is consciousness that does the doubting. First consciousness is needed so that then doubt can exist. There is something eternal about the mystery that is subjective and inward consciousness. Descartes thus demonstrated the necessary existence of what in existential phenomenology is called the transcendental dimension, which is the region of pure subjective consciousness. Doubt is the intellectual equivalent of what the emotions call anxiety. In other words, the *emotion* of anxiety reveals experientially the same phenomenon that the *concept* of doubt demonstrates intellectually—namely, the indestructibility, the eternity of consciousness, and the fact that its existence is logically necessary. This is one of the central discoveries of mankind; it is truly the alpha and the omega in understanding the solution to the problem of human meaning and fulfillment. It is philosophy's contribution to the well-being of mankind.

How, specifically, does anxiety reveal? Fear of loss is concern for a specific object. In that fear, the object is lost but the rest of the world remains; replacements are therefore possible. But anxiety is different; it is, as Heidegger has pointed out, the fear that the world itself will be lost. Anxiety is the dread that nothing remains, not even the world. Nothing remains *but the consciousness of total nothingness.* The concept of nothingness is needed in existentialism to describe and evoke the phenomenon of pure and eternal consciousness. It is a poetic metaphor; it is an important image.

The concept in the language of psychopathology that comes closest to this philosophical emotion of anxiety about nothingness is "separation anxiety." To a small child, the mother is the whole world. Remove the mother, and to the poor child all that remains in this world is a pure consciousness—his consciousness—reaching, reaching and reaching, and nothing else! The object of the reaching—in fact, all objects—have gone. The light of his consciousness is in search of an object that will reflect it. There is no object, because the mother is gone. There is only empty space. As a result, there is no luminosity at all to his world; only utter darkness, complete nothingness. That is the experience of dread, despair, and of ultimate anxiety. But it is also the experience of pure consciousness, for what remains when the whole world of objects has been erased is the absolute and empty reaching consciousness. Separation anxiety is like the ray of pure light that has lost all objects to illuminate. It is an arrow, pointing forever at nothing at all. In separation anxiety the ego is finally forced to look only upon itself, to see itself as it is, to comprehend its mysterious and saintly nature. Dread therefore is, strictly speaking, not an emotion at all; it is not the fear of an object. Dread is a philosophical event. Dread is a philosophical revelation. Dread is the nakedness of consciousness; its dress, which is the object, has been stripped away.

Naked consciousness, pure awareness, and objectless perception are unique experiences, alternately dreadful and euphoric. They are dreadful because the world is gone; but they are also euphoric, because consciousness remains—with all its extraordinary attributes of eternity,[1] timelessness, indestructibility, and the power of spontaneous and free creation.

Existential phenomenology transforms anxiety from an emotion, a mere disease, to a complex event containing within it a diamond core of priceless insight. And paradoxical though it seems, in philosophy, anxiety can lead to true peace of mind.

Ontological versus Neurotic Anxiety

One more word must be said to clarify the relationship between ontological and neurotic anxiety. The anxiety that discloses philosophic truths is ontological—that is healthy and authentic anxiety. Neurotic anxiety hides and distorts. Whereas ontological anxiety discloses the nature of pure consciousness, neurotic anxiety is often an expression of alienation. When the subjective and objective aspects of the field of consciousness are intentionally or dialectically related,[2] then there is in the organism a sense of peace, grace, and ease. This is my definition of health and authenticity. Under these circumstances, the anxiety level is very low. However, if that continuity of consciousness with its world

---

[1] Pure consciousness has some of the characteristics of God. This point is developed in Chapter 18 and 19 of *The Vitality of Death* and in my forthcoming book, *Is There an Answer to Death?*

[2] See the chapter on Metaphors for Consciousness.

is broken, then life is experienced as burdensome and troubled; it then becomes artificial, and it must be held together with raw willpower. Life is then bereft of meaning, for the artificial values upheld and constructions maintained are in constant threat of collapse. The relaxed sense of being natural and thus supported by the harmony between man and world is gone. The willpower that holds together the artificial construction is experienced as anxiety about the loss of truth and meaning. It is a most uncomfortable way to live and yet it is common. This is one aspect of neurotic anxiety. There is another way to describe the break of continuity in consciousness, a break that is called alienation.

Our bodily life occurs in the empirical realm, in the empirical or psychological ego, the body, the personality, and the emotions. These terms represent the objective pole of the field of consciousness. If our bodily existence has no access to the transcendental realm—the realm of pure, subjective consciousness—then there can *be* no field of consciousness, no self-transcendence, and no growth. That is the situation in neurotic anxiety.

A person who lacks the capacity for self-transcendence because the two poles of his field of consciousness are alienated from each other has a "constipated" or a withholding character structure: he does not transcend himself, emerge, or move. He has no time and no growth in his life. Such a person "kills" himself and others, in that he squelches the connection between the inner and the outer worlds. He kills authenticity in himself and is thus incapable of responding to it in others. If he is a parent, he will squelch self-transcendence in his children. Such a person deadens himself and those dependent on him by jailing and frustrating himself and others. He is unresponsive and, in general, unloving. This person is not in touch with his feeelings or his body. He fails himself in love and sex.

The themes on the Master Table concerned specifically with anxiety are C 1 and C 2.

Guilt

Another important existential emotion is guilt. The existential meaning of guilt can be evoked by such adjectives as *worthless, destroyed, unjust, unfair, shameful,* and *ashamed.* The ontological structure disclosed by the worldly emotion of guilt is freedom. In other words, the transcendental characteristic of man divulged by the empirical phenomenon of guilt is that freedom is the meaning of human existence, an integral aspect of the consciousness that I am. Guilt is the experience that I could have acted otherwise. Guilt therefore accompanies all of our choices, because to the extent that the options on which my decisions are based were real I could have meaningfully decided otherwise than I did. The gut realization of this fact of freedom is the experience of guilt. Guilt, to the degree that it reveals the existence of my inevitable freedom to me, can thus be a source of extraordinary strength and authenticity, for freedom is the experience of my creative powers and of my life's energy.

Technically speaking, guilt reveals to me two freedoms: the freedom of cathexis and the freedom of constitution. Freedom of cathexis means that I am free to identify myself with innumerable "objects," such as roles and self-definitions. I am free to choose my identity and to live out its destiny. Freedom of constitution is the potential for organizing the world in many different ways. Constitution gives me the freedom to attribute meanings and values to life-styles; it gives me freedom over my attitudes toward what I find in my living world. And it is only through the experience of guilt that I truly know, in the visceral sense, that I am free, and what all that freedom implies for success in human fulfillment.

Of what practical use is this revelation about my freedom? To know that guilt is freedom is to change weakness into strength, worry into self-confidence, and failure into success. To understand that guilt is proof of freedom is to move from paralysis to action, from being destroyed to being creative. In short, to find freedom in guilt is to overcome the paralysis of neurotic guilt and transcend to the creative power of existential guilt.

Physical Pain

Words that evoke the philosophical meaning of physical pain are mostly obvious expressions, such as *hunger, thirst, illness, headache, toothache, cramps, nausea,* etc.

In terms of the existential theory developed here, physical pain discloses the "cathexis of the body." Physical pain reveals the inner structure of the mysterious philosophical relationship that we (our consciousness) have to our body (our empirical ego). According to the field-of-consciousness theory of man, when we are in the act of perceiving our own bodies, then the ego is the subject and our body becomes an object to that ego. It is at this time of reflection that the details of our attachment to our bodies become visible. Pain is the experience of holding on to that attachment when the logic of the situation would be to let go. Medical tests, operations, dental work, injuries, and disease show us the dominion of the body over our spirits. We can reverse this relationship and view it from the inside of our consciousness, rather than from the outside of our body as does the medical practitioner.

How does it feel to be in the agony of pain? The body obtrudes itself on our consciousness. The body is so close to us that we have lost control over it. We certainly have lost the distance that spells sanity to us (principles A 2 and C 3 of the Master Table). We can therefore no longer enlist the help of the body to move around in the world. Think of an old-fashioned horse buggy. The driver controls the energy of his horses. The distance from him to the horses is needed for control. The experience of pain corresponds to the loss of that distance—the driver is on top of the horses or he is stampeded by them. Pain is also the horses going wild, ripping loose from the wagon, and dragging the driver with them. Then the pain is in holding on.

The pain will stop if the driver releases the reins. But so will the connection (cathexis) of consciousness and body, of subject and object poles in the field of consciousness. We cannot leave the body, because most of us have been taught that this means death and that death is evil. The pain is our holding on to our identification with the body. It is also our holding on to the organization which we have imposed upon it for the sake of the practical and individualized aspects of our life. When I am in pain I cannot walk, drive, work, cook, or travel. The direction of authentic consciousness, which in health moves from ego to body, has now been reversed or severed altogether.

In the agony of pain it makes sense to let go of the body—to relinquish it, to abandon it, to separate from it. We call this state death, anaesthesia, or unconsciousness. But we hold on to the body, literally, "for dear life." The exploration of physical pain discloses to us the answer to the important philosophical problem of the relation between the body and consciousness. And the answer given is not a conceptual one, but an empirical one. It is an answer based on the actual structure of experience, as that is experienced by the pained and observing consciousness.

How can these inward descriptions of the consciousness of pain aid us in the management of pain? The answers are found in withdrawal and perspective. Withdrawal means retreating into the space of consciousness away from the identification with the body. This life-style is the process of giving up the values of things and objects. Such an attitude becomes a viable alternative—it is the stoicism, asceticism, and monasticism of old—once it has been recognized as a legitimate human possibility. Withdrawal as a free solution to the problem of pain may also lead in selected cases to mild forms of self-hypnosis. Withdrawal can be brought about as follows: Concentrate on "looking at" the pain rather than "being" the pain. The farther away from the usually experienced locus of consciousness (between the eyes) the pain is, the easier it is to look at the pain rather than *being* the pain. Train yourself to be the observer of your pain. Do not identify yourself with the pain. Such dissociation cannot, however, be performed with fine discrimination for painful experiences only. It leads to indiscriminate dissociation not only from the pain but also from all actions and any pleasures.

For example, suppose you have an injured right foot. Think of the foot with its pain as being as far away from your center as possible. It helps if you imagine it to be the foot of someone else. The greater the experienced distance from your conscious center to the location of the pain, the more bearable the pain will be. But as you withdraw successfully, you will find that two accompanying conditions take place. You become generally inactive. If your foot is injured, withdrawal from the pain means also that you will do nothing to help yourself. To help yourself means deliberate action and body control. Philosophical withdrawal, on the other hand, means to give up that control. Furthermore, withdrawal means to relinquish our usual value-system. Withdrawal means to give up the value of health and even of life itself. It means adopting an I-don't-care attitude about everything. Philosophic withdrawal, therefore, carries a steep price, and should be used, like any anaesthetic, with great caution.

Let us now turn to the perspective that is achieved by recognizing through pain the mind-body relationship. Pain may not be allayed by being understood. But the meaning of life is grasped by that understanding. And once we are familiar with the larger designs of human existence, the threat of dying and the ruin of ordinary social values has been conquered. Philosophy makes man free. And that freedom gives him the sense to live splendidly with whatever objective realities are in his power.

Tragedy

The experience of tragedy in the life-world, or *Lebenswelt*, leads to an understanding of what I call the paradoxical, dialectical, polar, or intentional character of consciousness. This point was discussed in connection with the metaphors used to establish an image of the meaning of consciousness. The metaphors about the structure of consciousness in Chapter 1 were attempts primarily to depict the living and unconceptualizable character of consciousness. This bipolar "magnetic" field is called the intentionality of consciousness. It is this intentional and polar character of consciousness—a characteristic built into the very nature of reality itself—that surfaces in the emotional life of man as the experience of tragedy. Tragedy has always held a peculiar attraction for man. As an art form, it has been called "deep philosophy." The reason is that tragedy can reflect what is most real in being, the metaphysical basis of existence—in other words, the nature of consciousness itself.

The sense of tragedy is evoked by such words as *contradiction, paradox, sad, indecision, conflict, irresolvable, ambivalent, ambiguous,* etc. In tragedy—traditionally the highest art form—the intrinsic ambivalence of the ego-world, subject-object interaction is experienced strongly and directly. Tragedy leads to tears—not tears reminiscent of some puerile tantrum, but tears of insight and elevation, of depth and of resolution, rather than of mere frustration and anger. As is true of physical pain, the strength and the inspiration found in tragedy does not come from a resolution of the conflict or ambivalence that it represents. Instead, tragedy opens windows to the truth about man—a truth, compressed in theme C 14 of the Master Table, which transforms conflict from a debilitating problem to an invigorating challenge.

In some respects, tragedy is like a good marriage. To *resolve* a marital conflict is to *separate,* that is, to side with either husband or wife. To experience the oscillating conflict or the polar contrast as being the reality of the encounter between two human beings is to perceive the marriage as a success and as a higher level of human development than the unchallenged single status.

Tragedy is found in the unending *paradox* of wealth and poverty, peace and war, suffering and joy, justice and injustice, love and hate, success and failure, health and illness. These opposites have always existed and have puzzled suffering mankind. They will continue to plague us, for polarity is a name for the vibrancy of life itself. A non-polar consciousness is no consciousness at all.

Examples

It is important to bring an element of reality and experience into this paradox. We can contrast two products of human consciousness, two consequences of human decisions. There has been and always will be the lowest evil side by side with the highest good. It is the contrast that gives rise to the sense of tragedy. A newspaper story reports,[3]

BABY SURVIVES FOUR DAYS ALONE

An 18-month-old baby lay four days in her crib without food or water while the body of her murdered mother lay on the floor a few feet away.

Authorities are looking for the baby's father, an AWOL soldier from nearby Fort Ord.

The baby was severely dehydrated, and her kidneys were not functioning. She was taken to Ft. Ord Hospital and transferred to Letterman General Hospital in San Francisco. She was still being fed intravenously today but was in good condition.

[3] *San Jose News,* Friday, June 30, 1972, page 2. Reprinted by permission.

The discovery was made Wednesday night by the apartment managers and sheriff's deputies.

"If we had found her [the baby] Thursday morning, we would have had two deaths," said the Monterey County Det. Sgt.

He said she could not have lived another 12 hours.

The baby's 19-year-old mother was found on the floor of the bedroom in the apartment.

The baby apparently had been heard crying, but because there are several babies in the complex it could not be determined from which apartment the crying was coming.

The AWOL soldier's company commander had called at the home several times since Saturday in an attempt to get him to return to the base. He got no response to his knocks.

The last time the officer came to the apartment was Monday. He heard no sounds that day for the baby apparently had ceased crying by then.

The child's mother had been hit on the head with a blunt instrument, but it was not known immediately whether that was the cause of death because the body had begun to decompose.

The same world that produced the action of that husband-father also produced Ernesto Cardenal, who had the inspiration to write

All things love each other. All nature is oriented toward a *thou.* All beings that are alive are in communion with each other. . . .

All nature is in close touch and interwoven. All nature is in constant embrace. The wind which caresses me and the sun which kisses me, the air which I inhale, and the fish which swims in the water, the distant star and I who behold it: we are all in closest touch with one another. What we call the empty interstellar spaces are molded by the same matter that informs the stars, even though in a tenuous and rarefied way. The stars are but condensed forms of interstellar matter, and the entire universe is like one single immense star; and we all participate in this universe in one and the same rhythm—the rhythm of that universal gravity which accounts for the cohesion of an otherwise chaotic matter, a cohesion which joins the molecules together and causes certain particles of matter to unite at a definite place of the universe and which makes the stars what they are. And this unifying force is the rhythm of love.

Though we are all in close contact, we are all incomplete. This incomplete nature of ours strives unceasingly for greater perfection, and this striving we call evolution. The most perfect being in nature is man. And yet man, too, is incomplete; he, too, is imperfect and he, too, tends toward a *Thou:* he tends toward God. And when man loves God, he loves Him with the same ardent desire that animates all nature; he loves Him with the groaning of all creatures, with the immense perennial desire of the entire process of evolution. All creation sighs with us, as St. Paul says, in the travails of birth, the travails of the tremendous process of evolution.[4]

[4] *To Live Is to Love,* trans. Kurt Reinhardt (New York: Herder and Herder, 1972), pp. 21-22.

The authentic individual can live successfully in this world of unconscionable paradox and can find his meaning-giving destiny, his true challenge, in that paradox: Success means that life's struggle is set; it is struggle against the evil side of the paradox. We will die in the struggle, but we will have sanctified life in the process.

The management of tragedy is to descend from tragedy about tragedy (second-order tragedy) to simple and pure tragedy. Real tragedy makes man serious and purposeful. It makes him strong, gives him a proper sense of values and the capacity to make any life a noble one. Second-order tragedy is the nagging complaint about the existence of real tragedy; it is the weak complaining about the strong; it is the weak having contempt for the fulfilled. The authentic individual *wants* the intentionality of consciousness reflected in his world. He *wants* the movement of ambiguity. It is from the dialectical oscillation between subject and object that authentic love is born, because love is an eternally unresolved relationship between two incompatible and fully joined poles.

The Bible dreams about the end of paradox.

The lion will live with the lamb, and the panther will lie down with the kid, calf and lion cub will feed together, and a little boy will lead them. The cow and the bear will make friends, and their young will lie down together. The lion will eat straw like the ox, the infant will play over the cobra's hole, and the young child will put his hand into the viper's lair.[5]

Does Isaiah mean that paradox should end? that conflict will cease? that incompatible interests will be resolved or compromised? No. When we read this beautiful passage from the Old Testament we become sad, not joyous. Isaiah merely enhances our sense of tragedy. He tells us that love is beautiful; in fact, its beauty shines brightest when it becomes most painfully obvious to us that such bliss can never be. A living being that loves and protects, but does not live off of his surrounding nature will die of starvation. Conflict in nature reflects the oscillating dialectic, the wave phenomenon that is consciousness. Without its bipolarity, consciousness is not.

Man has no recourse; he must reach the realization that conflict is contrast and that contrast is what he himself would spontaneously create if he were God. What if there is disaster in your own personal life? Natalie's husband is a violent alcoholic who brings down catastrophe on her and the children. Should the wife and children say to themselves, "what beautiful tragedy? What inspiring destruction of life's most precious values"? Not at all! The problem itself comes from ignoring tragedy. Natalie has never integrated the meaning of tragedy into her life. She has consistently refused to live with ambiguity. Every

[5] Isaiah 11:6–8.

aspect of life has had to have for her an unambiguous solution. Because it is only when she recognizes that ambiguity and conflict are inevitable that she can gather her wits about her and take decisive action. Medical treatment, hospitalization, separation, or divorce—in other words, resolution of the problem—would have been the result of the integration of tragedy. She then would be saying, in effect, "Life is tragic; that insight makes me strong. I can therefore take courageous and rational action."

Some people live with too much tragedy, others do not have enough. Both types are inauthentic. The authentic individual has in his life the optimum amount of tragedy. This means that whatever tragedy there may be in his life, much or little, is for him the best possible living metaphor or practical symbol for the intentional or dialectical character that is his consciousness. In this way, an individual assumes responsibility for his life and chooses to make it meaningful.

Depression

Depression reveals to me that I have made the decision to say "no" to life. Adjectives that evoke the meaning of depression are *worthless, suicidal, unspirited, weak, tired, sad, blue, low, purposeless, pointless, disinterested, unconcerned,* etc. The discovery that one has said "no" to life, that one has chosen freely to deny the value of life itself, can come only to him who has the courage to feel himself into his depression, who can work through his grief. He must feel sadder than sad; he must experience the unbearable pitch-black hole, the incredible emptiness that exists at the conscious center of his being. Most of us are terrified to confront that emptiness, because we feel we cannot bear its destructive powers.

When a depressed individual comes close to reaching the nadir of his depression he is like a desert farmer drilling for a well in the dry soil. The deeper he drills the more discouraged he becomes. In the end he strikes water. He *must* strike water eventually because he is on top of an underground water table. Similarly, the depressed person is on top of his decision to say "no" to life, because the desolate emptiness is this very decision. If the self-disclosing individual drills deeply enough into his depression, he will strike the wellspring of that negative decision. He will discover and experience the free decision of continuously saying "no" to life. What then? Here is the important point: Once he is in touch with that decision, he has uncovered the freedom that can say "yes" to life as well as "no." Freedom is not conditioned, not determined. Freedom means we can say either yes or no and with equal facility. There is no reason or argument that points to either way. To say "yes" to life is to choose reason; then and only then do rational arguments become relevant. But they do not apply to the decision itself, because that reason-instituting decision has already been made and need not be made again. If we discover the freedom that is now saying "no" to life *we have also discovered the freedom that can say "yes" to life*. And this is the answer to depression. Depression will not disappear automatically; but we can *make* it disappear if we choose to do so. And only each individual ego can make that decision.

In other words, there exists no guarantee that once this freedom has been recovered, the individual will choose "yes" rather than "no" to life. Theme C 8 of the Master Table is a *desideratum;* but there is no guarantee that life will automatically be chosen. Death (real or symbolic) can be chosen with equal ease, or with as much difficulty as life. But if philosophy has an answer for the depressed individual and the suicidal person, it lies in the discovery that depression is a choice made with the same equipment and the same facility as is the joyous affirmation of life.

Depression thus reveals the dormant power for self-affirmation in all of us, and this uncovering is accomplished by revealing how in depression the power of self-denial is in use already. He who has reached these depths of his being is ready to handle successfully almost any depression.

Meaninglessness

A related type of pain is the sense of meaninglessness. It discloses the empty truth about the realm of values. We search for absolute values but in fact we must create our own. The discovery that the question of the meaning of life has no firm answers brings on the despairing sense of meaninglessness. However, meaninglessness also shows to each human being that he has the power of self-definition. He can create meanings for himself; he can set up values for his life. And above all he can, if he so chooses, set these values up in conformity with the field-of-consciousness theory of man. He can choose "natural" values, values in harmony with the field-of-consciousness theory of man, even though he is free to choose any value system whatever.

The sense of meaninglessness is associated with words such as *discouraged, indifferent, ennui, valueless, empty, bored,* and *disinterested.*

Except for the sense of meaninglessness, an individual will never understand that he has the Godlike capacity to establish a meaning for himself in life and that, while using it may be a mystery, a life of fantastic reality awaits him. In therapy, when a person is reborn or turns around to finally give his life meaning, he has reached the insight that in fact life is meaningless but for his own free and courageous choices.

Meaninglessness is the lack of a home; it is the expulsion from paradise, the fall of man. The question "What are my values?" echoes through the universe but is never answered by the universe. Answers are created by courageous freedoms. If we choose to be our bodies, if we choose to identify our meaning with our bodily nature (C 9 of the Master Table), if our self-image is biological, then we can be deeply touched by these words from the naturalist John Muir:

> Thousands of tired, nerve-shaken, overcivilized people are beginning to find out that going to the mountains is going home; that wildness is necessity; and that mountain parks and reservations are useful not only as fountains of timber and irrigating rivers, but as fountains of life. (1898)

This insight does not mean, however, that nature will *truly* be our meaning, fill the emptiness of our center. But it *does* mean that the real grief of our homelessness can be felt. Muir's perception of nature gives us a glimpse of the home we crave, of the home that we *might* have. It does not give us that home. But by taking us close, it makes the pain of our true homelessness—the meaninglessness of existence—grievously obvious.

Example

Here is a corporate business executive's powerful statement about meaninglessness in his life, taken from his journal. He is describing his marriage, which to him is the symbol of meaninglessness in his life:

> *Act One:* Setting—dismal first apartment.
> Enter the brick-mason of anti-sex
> wrong words—splat—"I didn't mean *that!*"
> empty look—splat—"What are you staring at?"
> frozen glare—splat—"Why are you laughing?"
> Up goes the wall—splat—splat—
> brick on brick—haphazardly laid—
>
> *Act Two:* Eyes stop meeting, fingers stop reaching, kisses turn to cheek-brushes
>
> *Act Two and a Half:* —Children—all great, all well.
> Need two parents
> Too proud to be less than two parents
>
> *Act Three:* Conversation
> Conversations are such fragile, fuzzy pups. Furry, damp-warm, blind.
> Trembling thirstily for the suck-warm, nectar-laden breast—but equally in need of the long, learned linguistics of the mother-tongue.

Grateful for the sibling rivalry.

Somehow fed, groomed, growing. The maturing conversation comes into focus from a fuzzy *there* to a laser-sharp *here*.

Well. That may be conversation-between-friends, but for *lovers*—an ephemeral, oral-genital intercourse is more the poetry of this petting. And in so exalted a setting, the empty gambit, the hollow openers, uttered because one's partner will remain silent forever if *someone* does not, in desperation, say *something*—the false replies—make a mockery of the entire relationship. Egos crumble and the wall goes higher splat—splat.

Act Four: Realization that there was more sex and love in three premarital months than twenty-three post-marital years—how many *thousand* calm, silent mornings, warm afternoons, slightly inebriated evenings wasted? How does love go? Let me count the nays.

Act Five: Children are going and soon the little old world takes another spin around the sun and the primal torture of having to face each other again, as in act one and two!

This time the partner-players know the plot; this time—no children fill the silent slots.

Final Curtain: A two-dimensional pale screen of wind-washed dunes—movement without change. Is this the life—good enough for ordinary purposes?

Is this why I am here?

Hell I'm still there and I'd say I can't get here from there.

Let me attempt a brief response in the spirit of a philosophical prescription.

When you feel life is meaningless because there is no love—poignantly described in the above letter—the first authentic response is protest. In that case you are determined to rebel against that aspect of fate and that facet of your human nature which troubles you. The second authentic response to meaninglessness is to recognize in that sense of meaninglessness the opportunity to be what you want to be, to establish for yourself the kind of life-world that only you can create. The answer to the problem of meaninglessness for this executive is to find in his own life situation specific and revolutionary ways to protest the meaninglessness he so clearly perceives. Because he describes his problem in a dramatic form, the participation in plays—as writer, actor or producer-promoter—might be a start toward meaning. Another start toward meaning may be a serious commitment to a psychotherapeutic relationship.

Still a third solution may be to now demand love from his wife by both persistent reasons and insistent feelings. A final possibility is to get busy searching for love elsewhere, if the days of protest and of therapy are over.

Loneliness

Loneliness—*aloneness, isolation, rejection, self-pity, alienation,* etc.— reveals the *uniqueness* of the ego. It discloses the meaning of themes C 4 and C 5 of the Master Table. Loneliness, although painful, leads to the realization that I cannot be replaced. I do my own suffering; no one can do that for me. But I also do my own enjoying; no one can be euphoric for me. I do my own eating and my own excreting; no one can do that for me either. I am unique; I am me; I am an individual. When I feel alone I discover not only the weighty burden but also the uplifting glory of the fact that I am myself and not somebody else. The "I am" experience is the beginning of an authentic and a fulfilling existence.

If I dislike loneliness, I am ignorant about my human nature and have false expectations of life. Once I understand man's nature, I recognize in my loneliness the high value of human existence: to be a unique individual. Once this is fully realized, being a unique individual is no longer a burden or a curse, nor a cause for self-pity. It means that my turn has come to play the game of life. And I have been waiting for that turn for a long time. I finally can live!

My loneliness tells me that I am special.

Frustration

The negative experience of frustration is allied to the anger-hostility-aggression syndrome. The experience of frustration can include, in addition to *anger* and *aggression,* such feelings as *bitterness, disgust, cruelty, hate, annoyance, destruction,* etc.

The ontological disclosure opened up by frustration is the reality of the Other in life. Frustration can be turned into love if we recognize that behind it lurks, at least in part, the childish desire to be alone with a fantasy world, the inability to confront the reality of the Other in existence.

To the philosophically ignorant, confrontation with the Otherness of the world is a disaster. Happiness seems to mean the elimination of the world, with its undeniable resistance to penetration. But the philosophically aware person understands that it is precisely the world's resistance which brings about the sense of reality proper. The shift from a fantasy world without resistance to a real world with insurmountable opposition is the conversion from the child to the adult, from the immature to the mature, from the dreamer to the realist, and from the inauthentic to the authentic. No one has stated the meaning of the Other better than Emily Dickinson when she wrote,

> Elysium is as far as to
> The very nearest room,
> If in that room a friend await . . .[6]

One major point remains in our discussion of the philosophic reduction of pain. And that is a program for the philosophical management of pain. To that point we now turn in the next chapter.

Remember:

1. Pain leads to truth.
2. *Anxiety and dread* disclose the existence and nature of your pure consciousness.
3. *Guilt* reveals to you that you have used your freedom.
4. *Physical pain* tells you that you love your body.
5. *Tragedy* discloses to you the polarities and ambiguities of life. They are but expressions of the natural polarity of your field of consciousness.
6. *Depression* reveals to you that you are now using your freedom to say "no" to life.
7. If you feel life is *meaningless* you are aware that you choose your own values, your own nature, and your self-definition.
8. Before you choose your values you must protest against the lack of values.
9. Your *loneliness* informs you that you are unique. You are not somebody else.
10. *Frustration* reveals to you that the world beyond your inward consciousness is real and is *there for you.*

[6] From *The Complete Poems of Emily Dickinson,* ed. by Thomas H. Johnson. Reprinted by permission of Little, Brown and Company.

13:

The Philosophic-Therapeutic Management of Pain

Mrs. Z. voluntarily requested hospitalization in a San Francisco institution because she had escalating suicidal fantasies, including impulses to jump, hang herself, and slash her wrists. She was anxious that these impulses and fantasies might come true. Mrs. Z. was twenty-three years old at the time.

She was placed under psychiatric observation and eventually told a tragic story indeed.

Her husband had insisted that she have sexual intercourse with another man while he watched. He found her a partner and, after some resistance, Mrs. Z. complied. The new relationship blossomed beyond what her husband had intended. One day, while Mr. Z. was at work, she and the man were in bed at the Z. residence. Mrs. Z.'s three-year-old boy, Douglas, wandered out of his room and into the back yard. She did not hear him because the door to her bedroom was locked. Douglas fell into the pool and drowned.

That was three months before Mrs. Z.'s voluntary admission to the hospital for fear of attempting suicide. During that three-month period Mrs. Z. suffered periods of severe depression and ferocious anxiety.

Mrs. Z. received philosophically oriented therapy—that is, she went through an intensive existential analysis—and following is an outline of the process. It is a summary overview of the existential elements of extensive and long-term therapy.

An Authentic Problem

Mrs. Z. had a problem that meets the two criteria of what is needed for a problem to lend itself to existential therapy: her problem was a genuine paradox, an authentic conflict. There was (1) *no solution* and (2) its *agony* was unbearable. The conflict was between life and death; between affirming life, based on the fact that she recognized the values of existence, and denying life, which she had already done, at least in her opinion of herself. Her life-style had been utterly inauthentic and that inauthenticity expressed itself in her world (Master Table theme A 3). Her sexual perversion—in which she really did not wish to participate—meant she allowed her husband to choose for her in a region that is her province exclusively. She chose to permit her husband to define her. She bartered her freedom to define herself for his at best ephemeral promise not to abandon her. That choice was a decision for inauthenticity, a choice for death. But Mrs. Z. now realizes that she made that choice against life freely.

The death by drowning of her son was a dramatic reflection in the objective world of the selling out of her freedom in the subjective world. When she sold her freedom her world died; the real values of her world were thereby destroyed. In technical language, when her transcendental ego sold its freedom (chose to deny its freedom), the empirical ego died. And because the empirical ego is the worldly environment in which she lives and which she has constructed, it died in the form of her precious child. (That is also one theme in John Updike's novel *Rabbit, Run*.)

Mrs. Z. was in conflict. Her guilt and her anxiety were symptoms of her underlying conflict. She chose life to the extent that she was still living and that she voluntarily had herself committed to avoid possible suicide. But she also chose death in that she was responsible for the destruction of her only child. She chose death in that she lived in an intolerable marriage, and in that she lived as an object to be used by her husband, rather than a subject to be encountered by another authentic inwardness. She chose death in the sense that she *let* her life happen rather than *made* it happen.

Her problem was agonizing because she was now in touch with the region of human freedom where choice or decision-making can no longer be postponed, avoided, or repressed. The tragedy of her life forced upon her the truth about human existence.

There is one choice that is not symbolic, but literal; it is a choice that cannot be postponed for even a fraction of a second, because its postponement is already a choice. It is the choice underlying all other

choices. Each person is confronted every living moment with this tremendous dilemma: "Do I choose life or do I choose death? Do I choose
to say 'yes' to life or do I choose to say 'no' to life?" Mrs. Z. had reached,
fortunately and unfortunately, the agony of that ultimate philosophic
depth. She was truly in the grip of a crisis. She was confronted with
principle C 8 of the Master Table.

The Therapist's Philosophic Posture

For successful existential therapy to take place the therapist must himself have an authentic philosophic attitude. Mrs. Z.'s therapist felt
strongly that his patient was not sick, but healthy; that she was not mal-
adjusted, but confronted with a philosophical reality. He decided to
deal with her problem at the level of its philosophic depth and not on
that of its symptomatic surface. Specifically, the therapist felt that Mrs.
Z.'s problem was an expression of the authentic structure of existential conflict itself, and that consequently her problem had no solution
and all search for it would thus be futile. Solution would have meant
that the life-death choice had a permanent and unilateral answer. To
insinuate that such an answer exists would be a deception. To recognize
that conflict as ontological and authentic—even at the unbearable level
at which Mrs. Z. experienced it—is the truth about man. She can live
with it. We all live with it, and are stronger and more real for living
with it. And she can reconstruct her life on her strengths thus discovered.

Furthermore, Mrs. Z.'s problem, her therapist recognized, was but a
metaphor—a powerful one, needless to say—for the total ontological
structure of the field of consciousness itself. Her problem is an offshoot
of human nature itself. Her agonizing dilemma, between life and death,
depression and joy, failure and success is but a blurred photograph of
consciousness itself. Mrs. Z.'s problem reflects the incompatibility between the subjective and the objective regions of the field of consciousness that is the universe. We here see a combination of principles A 1
and C 14 of the Master Table.

Her problem also reflects the meaning of freedom, which is always
confronted with at least two alternatives from which to choose (principle C 7). And the existential message is that the truth makes you
strong. If it should happen that the truth makes you weak—as it did
Mrs. Z. at the time of her admission to the hospital—it is because of
an inability to accept philosophic realities. Had she accepted earlier the
dialectical ambiguities of human nature and her consequent responsibility, she would not have been in the mess in which she found herself.
But she was able to accept the present chaos of her life as a further

expression of man's dialectical ambiguities. Once that was done, she found the strength to reorganize her life and to assume responsibility for its betterment.

Mrs. Z. was now ready for the lessons of existential philosophy. Thus, her therapist recognized genuine hope and good news beneath all her despair and anxiety, depression and guilt. Why? Because she was at that moment in touch with the freedom of her consciousness and with its bipolarity. *These are the resources for authenticity in all human beings.*

These existential ideas were always kept alive in the mind of the therapist and gave direction to his strategy in treating Mrs. Z.

The Message for the Patient

It was made clear to Mrs. Z. in many ways and using many of the techniques of psychotherapy, that the point she then reached in her therapy —the experiences of freedom and of contradiction—was really a condition of health and authenticity. She reached a point where mature philosophic self-knowledge was not only possible but forced itself on her. She was not sick: she had reached the center of her authenticity, her health. Her problem was the surface appearance of a universal philosophic truth. She had to wrestle with that truth not just for herself but, heroically, for all mankind. The therapist's attitude as well as his words conveyed this message.

The therapeutic consequences to Mrs. Z. were these: that she must rest on her anguish, dwell on it, "get into it." She must train herself, with the aid of her therapist, to let herself go completely into her anguish by relaxing fully and meditating on her agony. She must get in touch with the full extent of her anxiety. She was reassured repeatedly that no worse disaster would occur; she was physically protected in the hospital setting. In fact, she is already—at this moment in her life—confronting "the worst possible disaster"—that is, the emptiness of her existential freedom and the conflict between life and death. Mrs. Z. can now live confidently in the full exposure of her feelings of grief. The healthiest of all experiences, the experience that yields the maximum amount of strength, is the experience of forcing oneself to face the terrifying abyss of freedom, the horrid emptiness of ambiguity. Because once one has forced himself to face that fully one knows that he has faced *successfully* the ultimate threat; the indestructibility of human consciousness (theme C 6) will have flashed into awareness.

When she is thus comfortably close to her feelings and safe at the same time, Mrs. Z. goes through violent and powerful expressions of emotion. She screams and weeps, she flails her arms and kicks her feet. She rages and she pounds. All of this is encouraged, as it would be in rage-reduction or primal-scream therapy. These feverish outbreaks of emotion show to Mrs. Z. herself the affective or feeling content of her existential discovery, of her philosophic nature—that is, of the freedom of her consciousness. An existential-philosophic truth can be a fantastically emotional experience. She has discovered that to be human is to face this terror and to discover that such a confrontation is both *possible* and *strength-giving*.

The major obstacle to this kind of existential therapy is the anxiety it produces in the therapist, not what it does to the patient.

The Existential Crisis

The next stage for Mrs. Z. is to begin making her peace with the existential freedom and existential paradox that she has now confronted within herself. She now feels right about the terror, because the second-order pain is gone. She no longer feels anxious about her anxiety or guilty about her "abnormality" or neurosis. And she feels right about the terror because she has seen that it cannot touch the inward consciousness which she is. She feels strong and human; she has rejoined the healthy mainstream of mankind. She is now working for all of us: as she resolves her problem she also resolves it for history. She has become a philosopher.

There exists a state of being in which a person can accept the most intolerable in himself and in others. Mrs. Z. has achieved that state. And that state is a more noble condition than suicide, which was her earlier response to that same intuition. Let us examine how this matter worked itself out in Mrs. Z.'s existential therapy.

Her therapist led her to fierce and determined suicidal thoughts. Her guilt and sense of worthlessness were so intense that the ultimate act of aggression against the body or the person that lived so sinfully was a reasonable release. Self-murder was the logic of the heart. Mrs. Z. dwelt on that stage for three full months in her therapy. Now comes the supreme act, the dénouement. Can she and will she say "yes" to life in the presence of all that nothingness? Paul Tillich defines God as the power to resist nonbeing. Mrs. Z. is face to face with nonbeing—her guilt, her evil, her depravity, as she sees it. Is nonbeing to win and determine her decision for her?

Mrs. Z. reached her existential crisis. The therapist had to stay out of it. The final decision was hers and not that of the therapist. And here the therapist must be a philosopher. The therapist is professionally and legally obligated to save the life of his patient, even if that would lead to a vegetable existence for the latter. In a manner of speaking, the philosopher has no such professional or legal obligation—although he may well have chosen to save a life at all costs as his personal ethical commitment. The philosopher can thus witness—and that is all; just witness, not direct—the agony of the free choice of his patient. The philosopher must accept the patient's choice.

Mrs. Z. decided, without prompting and without reference to instinct, that *in spite* of the depravity of her empirical ego she would say "yes" to life. At that moment of crisis (*kairos*) she became recreated, rechosen, and redefined: she reconstituted and reconstructed herself. She became a different person altogether. A new individual was born. If you walk uphill against a rainstorm you feel strong and real, as the sharp wind whips your face and the freezing rain numbs it. To say "yes" to life against the death of her only child because of her irresponsible neglect has the same kind of strength-giving significance. It is difficult to depict this extraordinary and refreshing experience. Yet it is this possibility—which is universal in all of us but made conscious only to a privileged few—that places human beings outside of the order of nature. It truly makes us supernatural.

Mrs. Z. must hold onto her experience and her insight—the noble strength won from ignoble adversity. It is right that she affirm the glory of her life in spite of and against all she despises.

Is This the Best of All Possible Worlds?

Mrs. Z.'s explorations into her inwardness have now completely transcended any psychological problem. She is no longer a patient in a hospital, a social pariah, but she has joined the ranks of the world's philosophers. Philosophy is the most ancient of the healing arts. It occupies itself with the ills of being human. She is now ready to come to terms with the problem of evil.

At this stage of her existential "treatment" (her "philosophical development" is a better expression), Mrs. Z. developed a spiritual, mind- and consciousness-centered world-view sharply different from the materialistic view she had absorbed from our culture. Her new values were connected with the eternal aspects of human consciousness. Her physical and psychological tensions diminished because her involvement with the world became relaxed and even somewhat aloof rather than compulsive and desperate. She now dealt with problems in a global rather than a particularized way. She moved from what had been a mechanical approach to the problems of human existence to a humane approach. Her world-view approached the model of Oriental philosophies—a great peace came over her. It was a peace based on true insights about the nature of man and not on artificial tranquilization. It was an infinite peace based on sharpened and penetrating vision rather than on blocked and dulled sensitivities. She moved away from the object-centered philosophies of the West to the subject-centered philosophies of the East. She experienced a change in attitude, perception, and interpretation. She felt her anguish had been due to blindness and ignorance about the real nature of man and the world in which he exists. She had "converted" from a ghost-in-a-machine theory of man to a field-of-consciousness theory of man. What began as antidepressive therapy concluded with one of the great visions of philosophy.

Involved here is the discovery that this is, as Leibniz held, the best of all possible worlds. Only when one identifies one's consciousness with a cosmic consciousness will this be the best of all possible worlds. But this view, for Mrs. Z., can be held only if she does not identify herself exclusively with the fate of a small region of this world: her body, her husband, her boyfriend, or her dead child. Only when her fate is the fate of the universe, only when she thinks of herself as truly a child of the universe will this world—with all the injustices that it visits upon man—be to her the best of all possible worlds.

Let us now turn to a final philosophic-therapeutic illustration: how existential philosophy can help manage death.

14:

The Existential Meaning of Death: A Response to a Public Health Nurse

Death is the most dramatic reminder of the permanent presence of negation in life. This examination is a response to a question raised by a nurse attending one of my seminars.

The Management of Death

Question: "I am a public health nurse. I work in particular with dying children (leukemia, cancer) and with their parents, but also with dying oldsters in general. How can existential philosophy help me help my patients?"

Answer: Rule number one is for you to achieve authenticity in the area of death yourself. You must understand, first, the full *theoretical* spectrum of the existential philosophy of death and dying and you must learn, second, to fully integrate these intellectual insights into your *experience* and into your life. In other words, to help your patients you yourself must be ready to die today.

But there is more: You must also be able to die with dignity as if you were now a child. Furthermore, you must be capable of managing your life as the parent of a dying and then a dead child; and finally you must be able to die as an old person, even in agony and loneliness. Once you are ready, you can help your patients.

If you have gone through the intellectual work of understanding and then through the emotional work of coming to terms with these issues, then the practical question of how to help your patients is relatively minor. Most of what is then needed is for you, as an authentic person, to make yourself available to them. Individuals who seek mere *techniques* for the management of the emotionally stricken may in reality wish to bypass any personal involvement with and personal commitment to the afflicted patient. However, it is precisely this ability to make a commitment to the patient that will help him. When a nurse seeks techniques she is in effect asking to be transformed into a health machine that will "cure" philosophical or existential ills automatically, forgetting that what heals philosophic ills such as fear of inevitable death is love, devotion, and commitment. The personal relationship and not the technique has the healing powers. The belief that a purely technological approach to inevitable death is even theoretically possible is evidence of total inauthenticity; it is proof of having completely misunderstood the nature of man, especially the dimension of intimacy, of intersubjectivity.

Rule number two is to understand the philosophical elements in the management of death. These make up the heart of an existential personality theory and can be summarized as follows.

An individual whose life is relatively uneventful will manage death with modest success if he adopts the first solution to what in existential philosophy I call "the paradox of self-transcendence"—i.e., the conscious *repression* of philosophical themes. Many people go through life easily without ever seriously contemplating death. You, as a public health nurse, have made the contemplating of death your profession, the center of your life.

Parents

What does the knowledge of death do to the healthy individual? Only when that question is answered can we deal with the sick. In your case, the healthy ones are the *parents* of dying children. To them, the philosophical truth about death means the discovery of (1) life's true values and (2) life's true limits.

Confronted with death—any death whatever—that of a pet, a child, a grandparent, a stranger, or your own—an individual immediately recognizes what values are important and which are not. For the nurse speaking to parents, this insight means she should focus not only on the values lost but also on the values remaining, as well as those still to be created. For instance, there may be other children—if not, the parents might have or adopt additional children. The values of being a child and of being a parent remain. In fact, the death of a child immeasurably enhances the values of *all* children and of *all* parents. The death of a child sanctifies the values of childhood and parenthood. True, the love for the new children can never make up for the lost child. But new children are loved more intensely, warmly, and meaningfully with a love that is nurtured on the soil of the dead child. And that places in sharp focus the divine value of a human consciousness.

Furthermore, the death of their child represents limitation for the parents. Death is coming; that is a fact. No one and nothing can change that fact. And that fact is bad; in fact, it seems to be the worst that can happen to anyone. It is the fate and nature of man to be condemned by these boundaries, these impenetrable barriers. To be human is to be (unfairly) limited in this way. But to be fully human is also to genuinely want to live with these boundaries: that is the difference between the infinity of God and the finitude of man.[1] Wanting to be human is wanting to be limited. And the ability to confront death is the proof of that want.

How can a nurse get these abstract philosophic ideas across to the living needs of the parents of a dying child? She can focus on the reality of the situation. She can emphasize that the child *will* die and call attention to the fact rather than simply help them escape the reality that death is indeed a tragedy and a terrible injustice, without redemption. She can help make clear to the parents that they, as human beings, are absolutely limited, that we all are the prisoners of our own humanity. She must avoid all statements that indicate there is hope for the child or that his death is not as tragic as was really thought. The burial of the child is necessary—painful as it is for the family—to make clear to all the absolute finality of death. That finality must be faced and confronted even before the death of the child. Absolute limits and impenetrable barriers define our humanity.

The nurse might help by calling attention to *other* limits in their and others' lives. The parent himself may have lost a parent, or he may even have lost his own childhood in a war or depression. He may have lost the opportunity for education or for the pursuit of a talent. To those who are well, the survivors of the dead, a philosophical analysis of death enhances seriousness about life by eliciting man's true values and realistic limits.

But this approach is for the living, not for the dying, because these comments regarding the confrontation with our limits are principally for the healthy. Death vitalizes only those who can reasonably expect to still do some substantial and heady living. Those who are about to die must be treated far more carefully and on separate principles. Death has a different meaning for those who know they are about to die than for those who believe they have much life left in them. In deter-

[1] We can think of God and man as part of a continuum: the eternal struggle between the finite and the infinite which is the mystery of existence. The infinite chooses to be finite while still retaining the desire for infinity.

mining what approach to take, the crucial question that the nurse must answer is, "What is my patient's concept of death?"

Since no one living has died, for each of us the death of our subjective consciousness is but a speculative belief. It is this belief that makes us human.

Immortality

An old person must be given serious hope in the indestructibility of consciousness. That can be done through philosophical analysis or religious metaphor. The dying patient who has had time to prepare himself is usually peaceful and even joyous. He experiences the peace of one who knows that he is an industructible consciousness not necessarily involved with the world. The dying person who is reconciled in this fashion has become in effect the saintly ascetic revered by all the world cultures in all periods of history. He participates in his death.

You would like to be able to tell your dying patients "Death is not the end." As a nurse dealing with the dying, you hope that the notion of immortality—that is, the idea that consciousness is an Eternal Now and that time is outside the consciousness, an object to consciousness rather than an integral part of consciousness itself—can be supported philosophically. Can you accept that? Can you accept it theoretically? Practically and feelingly? Your answer, as a nurse, has to be "yes," if you are to be fully effective.

Here is a letter from a friend that, in the context of Alcoholics Anonymous, begs to substitute the philosophical idea of the indestructible consciousness for the religious belief in immortality:

> Dear Dr. Koestenbaum:
>
> Just some quick comments about the chapter in your book [*The Vitality of Death*] about "Phenomenology of Religion." As you know, because of my AA training I have come to depend a great deal upon a "Higher Power" to get sober and to stay sober in AA. For 10 years this "Higher Power" has been represented by my "AA Group." I have not been able to accept the "God Concept" or the "Spiritual Thing" because of my disastrous 16 years of Catholic schooling.
>
> I am now ready to accept intellectually and emotionally your phenomenological concept of "my pure subjective consciousness" as my "Higher Power." However, I would like your personal comments to me about this—perhaps on the phone later this week, if possible.

The writer suffers, literally, from the "death of God," the malady that was first described by Nietzsche. He hopes the existential notion of pure consciousness can serve as substitute for his lost but needed God. But a concept alone cannot take the place of a living experience and vibrant reality. He needs a friend, one who cares and who loves, one who is permanently and fully available—a person who should have been but was not present in his childhood. He needs evidence of another consciousness connected to his consciousness. It is not enough for him to understand the principles of existential philosophy; he must also experience their meaning in the manner in which he lives. Existential philosophy cannot be understood fully in one's study—any more than one can live fully there. Understanding also means action and above all, relations with people, commitment to people—interactions of consciousnesses. That is where the nurse can enter in. She is the conscious contact, the intersubjective presence, because she has made a commitment to the patient until he dies!

Time

The child, however, does not really know that he is dying. He does sense the anxiety of his parents and thus fears something dreadful, even worse than death itself. His life must nevertheless continue normally, unchanged, with hope, tenderness, and the full presence and availability of the consciousness of his parents.

When a child has hope he possesses in effect an unadulterated sense of time. To be alive in the world means to have become time. Time is always directed into the future. To experience time as a continuum that is rooted in the present and uses the past in order to point to the future is the authentic experience of time. A dying child must retain the sense of authentic time—the future for him must always exist. It is the privileged challenge of the parents and the nurse to create an emotional and educational environment for the child in which he can have a future- and growth-oriented life. The child must continue to enjoy a humanistic education: literature and the arts, philosophy and religion, and above all, the love and intimacy of other human beings.

Shakespeare expressed himself masterfully on the subject of death when he wrote:

> Cowards die many times before their deaths,
> The valiant never taste of death but once.
> Of all the wonders that I yet have heard,
> It seems to me most strange that men should fear,
> Seeing that death, a necessary end,
> Will come when it will come.

> *Julius Caesar,* Act II, scene ii.

Remember:

These are the basic points to remember in the management of death.

1. To help others with death you must first have come to terms with your own death, both intellectually and emotionally.

2. Specifically, you must have made your peace with four possible kinds of death:
   a. your death now;
   b. your death if you were now a child;
   c. the death of your child or a loved one now;
   d. your death as an old and ailing person.

3. Techniques to help the dying are meaningless, because death is a philosophical problem rather than a medical one. Consider that there is no cure for death!

4. To help the dying you must understand the existential ideas regarding death.

5. Many people repress the fact of death.

6. Knowledge of death helps us understand the true values of life.

7. Knowledge of death helps us understand the true limits of human existence.

8. It is necessary to point out the increase in the remaining values and obligations because of the death of a loved one.

9. It is necessary to point out the deep meaning of the finitude of man made apparent by the death of a person.

10. The question of the eternity of consciousness should be raised with adults directly and with children indirectly.

11. The dying should be helped as far as possible to retain hope and a sense of time that moves into the future.

Conclusion:

What Is
a Philosopher?

The role of philosophy and of the philosopher has not changed since Socrates. Professional philosophers are rare; that is, there are few of them. They often are lonely, rejected and frequently they are completely, even deliberately, misunderstood. What the philosopher has to say is not a truth like a chemical equation, which exists safe at a distance from the living human libido, but is an individual statement, a personal commitment wrought out of him through the strenuous agony of reality itself.

When a philosopher practices philosophy he is more like a prophet than a professional. He must be an individual and act as an individual, for he is not protected by any guild. His essential and individual being is on the line. He is not guarded by a group—a profession, a school, a legal entity, a religion or a tradition. He cannot hide. He is himself and he is alone. And in so living he cannot help himself. He wants to be no martyr: he does not relish persecution; nor does he desire to be misunderstood. But his commitment to be a genuine individual, a true human being—not a carbon copy of what happens to be popular or safe—is but a statement of the universal human essence.

The role of the philosopher in America is not unlike the role of the poet and the novelist in Russia. He, as was Socrates, is the conscience of all individuals. He is not a conscience in the sense of setting moral rules, not at all. The philosopher is the conscience of men because he reminds them of the nature of their humanity. And when people are confronted with the ultimate philosophical realities of their human nature they run away, deny, attack, ignore or destroy. Why? Because much of what goes under the name of living is really dying. For many, the project of life becomes how to maximize self-deception. For others, life is really ignorance of life. And when confronted with their assumptions, people are threatened and defend themselves with their ignorance. The wages of integrity are injustice.

Why is philosophy threatening? The philosopher thinks to the roots. That means he first uncovers assumptions and then questions them. He is honest in his work. He is both logical and empirical, both rational and intuitive, both thoughtful and observant. He is both a logician and a scientist, a mathematician and an artist. When the questioning of assumptions is integrated into a person's life, then the experience is more like an earthquake or a tornado than a game of chess or a crossword puzzle. When the question becomes "What are *my* assumptions?" then the desperate defenses of the psychological organism close ranks for a last stand.

What Is Personalized Education in Philosophy?

Let me now be specific. What is personalized education in philosophy? Education in philospohy is the effort and the desire to help an individual understand himself philosophically. It was to this goal that Nietzsche and Kierkegaard devoted their lives. Education in philosophy is to help an individual see what is going on in his life in the area of his basic philosophical issues and assumptions. Personalized education in philosophy is to discover, in one's own existence, the meaning of life. Personalized education in philosophy is to experience the power of these questions: "What is the meaning of my life?" "*Does* my life have any meaning?" "*Should* my life have meaning?" "What do I search for, in the quest for meaning?" "Is there any meaning to the question of my meaning?"

I ask "Is it not dangerous, or at least unethical, to pretend that one can help an individual with his philosophical agony, with the problem of giving significance, reality and meaning to his life, by using, not the science of man (which is philosophy) but the science of animals (which is biology and physiology) and the science of sand, stones and water (which is chemistry and pharmacology)?" Fortunately, most individuals in the healing arts are people first and professionals second, guaranteeing in this manner that in truly helping others they are doing philosophy through the language of one of the natural or life sciences. Philosophy is not primarily concerned with mental illness. Personalized education in philosophy begins with a healthy person and helps him through the universal human stresses present even in the most successful of people: love, independence, death, suffering, frustration, compassion and responsibility.

The philosophical questions that are brought to the philosophical consulting room are questions about both the nature and the authenticity of consciousness. They are questions not of consciousness in general, but of *my* consciousness in particular. It is unethical, irrelevant and even damaging to handle the problems of the nature and the health of consciousness (or of the "spirit," if one prefers) without recognizing the deeply philosophic character of these issues. These questions cannot be dealt with in terms of childhood experiences or behavior modification. The damage done in handling philosophical questions without philosophy is that the student or patient will think he is dealing successfully with, for example, the problem of the meaning of life, while in actual fact the true issue may never be even remotely touched. Fortunately, again, many a person in the healing professions—because he is an outstanding human being in his own right—when dealing with a healthy person, performs a philosophic function and task, even while not being fully conscious of it and deliberate about it.

Personalized education in philosophy means that an individual comes to terms in his own personal life with such philosophic problems as the relationship between the mind and the body, thought and feeling. He comes to grips with the question of human freedom, not in abstract and universal terms, but in his own life and his own experience. In personalized education in philosophy, the student confronts the issue of the reality of other minds, which is the phenomenon of encounter, and with it the corresponding question of ethics in human relationships. In personalized education in philosophy the individual discloses to himself the characteristics of his own consciousness—how it constructs meanings or how it fails to do so. These are epistemological issues made personal.

Personalized education in philosophy concerns itself also with the question of an individual's own personal death and how to manage it. It deals with the relation of the individual with whatever the word "God" stands for in his life. Personalized education in philosophy deals furthermore with the meaning of love—one of the most crucial philosophical themes. But again the concern is not with love-in-general but with the meaning of love in *my* life. Finally, personalized education in philosophy concerns itself also with the choice of values. We must all live, and raise our children, by values that we believe to be true. This is not an academic question; it is a personal one. It is not a question of mind nor is it one of the body. It is a question that vibrates through the total human being. And each of us is condemned to answer.

The philosopher has spent his life wrestling, alone, with these questions. And we are all philosophers.

INDEX

Adaptability, 44–45
Anxiety, 150–53
Art of Loving, The (Fromm), 96
Asceticism, 97–98
Authenticity profile, interpreting, 48–61
Autobiography (Russell), 2–3, 32

Baer, Louis Shattuck, 131–32

Cardenal, Ernesto, 96, 158
Center, the, 68–69
Comet theory of objects, 13
Commitment, 44, 67
Consciousness
  authenticity profile, interpreting, 48–61
  journal-writing, 93–106
  Master Table, 37–45, 66–73, 85, 106, 153–54, 157
  metaphors for, 11–26
  self-development, program for, 85–92
  two concepts of, 27–36
Constitution, 41, 144–45
Contradiction, 45
Crime, 19, 34–36

Death, 42, 72, 161
  management of, 173–78
Depression, 160–61
Descartes, René, 151
Dickinson, Emily, 165
Dread, 150–52

E-I-F Journal, 93–106
Encounter, 97, 99
Eternity, 43, 68
Existential family counseling, 13–16
Existential integration, 100–105
Existential personality theory, 37–45, 86

Fantasies, 94–99
Field-of-consciousness theory of man, 12–13, 19, 21, 25, 33, 34, 40
Finitude, desirability of, 42, 144, 146–49
Forgiveness, 97, 99
Freedom, 24–25, 43, 71, 74–75, 154, 167, 168
Freud, Sigmund, 79
Fromm, Erich, 96
Frustration, 164–65

Ghost-in-a-machine theory of man, 18–24, 33–36
Growth, 45
Guilt, 63–64, 73–84, 138, 139–40, 153–54

Home, 3–7, 162
Honesty, 104–5
Hope, 66–67
Husserl, Edmund, 11

Immortality, 176–77
Independence, 77–78
Individuality, 42
Insight Application Form, 85–92, 106

Journal-writing, 93–106

Kelbach, Walter, 19, 34–35
Kierkegaard, Sören, 180

Lance, Myron, 19, 34–35
Liebniz, Gottfried von, 172
Life, 43, 71
Loneliness, 164
Love, 20, 30–33, 44, 72, 96–97

Master Table, 37–45, 66–73, 85, 106, 153–54, 157
Meaninglessness, 161–64
Muir, John, 162

Negation, meaning of, 143–44
Neurotic anxiety, 152–53
Nietzsche, Friedrich Wilhelm, 176, 180

Okamoto, Kozo, 19
Ontological anxiety, 152–53
Ontological pain, 138
Other, the, 144–46, 164–65

Pain, 42, 72
  defined, 128–37
  depth of, 138–49
  philosophic-therapeutic management of, 166–72
  types of, 150–65
Pain Test, 107–27, 150
Philosophy, 1–10, 179–81
Physical pain, 154–56

Reality, 44
Reflection, 42, 66, 68, 69
Responsibility, 41
Reverence, 43
Roles, 21–23
Russell, Bertrand, 2–3, 32
Ryle, Gilbert, 18

Self-concept, 27–36, 85–86
Self-development, program for E-I-F Journal, 93–106
  Insight Application Form, 85–92
Self-disclosure, 41, 138
Self-reliance, 42, 70, 72
Self-transcendence, 153
Shakespeare, William, 177
Socrates, 78, 179

Terrorism, 19
Tertullian, 136
Tillich, Paul, 170
Time, 45, 177
To Live Is to Love (Cardenal), 96
Tragedy, 156–60
Two selves, 40

War, 19